Strange Fire Holy Fire

Strange Fire Holy Fire

Exploring the Highs and Lows of Your
Charismatic Experience

Michael J. Klassen

BETHANYHOUSE
Minneapolis, Minnesota

Published by Bethany House Publishers
11400 Hampshire Avenue South
Bloomington, Minnesota 55438

Bethany House Publishers is a division of
Baker Publishing Group, Grand Rapids, Michigan.

Printed in the United States of America

ISBN   978-0-7642-0549-1

Library of Congress Cataloging-in-Publication data is available for this title.

Acknowledgments

Winston Churchill once wrote:

> Writing is an adventure. To begin with, it is a toy and an amusement. Then it becomes a mistress, then it becomes a master, then it becomes a tyrant. The last phase is that just as you are about to be reconciled to your servitude, you kill the monster and fling him to the public.

The one plight more perilous than writing a book is being married to the person writing a book. Kelley, you are a saint for dutifully serving as my sounding board. You listened intently when the idea for this book was a toy and an amusement, and you hung in there with me when it became my tyrant. Thank you. You're more than my wife, you're the love of my life! Anna, Allie, and Marina, thank you for enduring the many hours I barricaded myself in my office. I can't imagine having more wonderful daughters than the three of you.

James and Harriet Klassen (whom I affectionately call Dad and Mom), you modeled grace to many as you guided our family through the charismatic movement. Throughout your lives, but especially during the days of the Jesus People Movement, you have impacted countless people. Thank you for embodying a living faith that proves we can love God with our heart *and* our mind. My sisters, Lori Aguiar and Lisa Schalla, shared similar experiences to mine, yet have sifted the chaff from their charismatic experience without becoming bitter. I love you both and feel so fortunate to live close to you.

These people introduced me to a relationship with Jesus during my formative years: Lou Montecalvo, Jerry Schoel, Lloyd Apodaca, Pete Rutt, Charles McPheeters (he's probably doing his Freddie Feathers routine in heaven right now!), Mike and Jan Bird, Doug and Marti Toller, Phil Abeyta, Bob and Linda Grant, Bill and Mimi Grant, Jerry and Kathy Stevens, Tom Brock, and Walt Pegram. Later, Charles Blair, Oral Roberts, Ron McIntosh, Steve Fulp, John Wimber, Father Sam Gantt, Jim Maust, and Peter Hiett built on their foundation. Thank you for allowing God to use you to imprint the life of Jesus on me!

While I was in seminary, I wasn't sure if I wanted to be associated with the charismatic movement anymore. Dr. Walter Hollenweger showed me how to sift through the problems and promises of being a charismatic. Your vibrant faith, passionate prayers, and love for Jesus renewed my faith—and it was only a two-week class!

The people of Lookout Mountain Community Church in many ways became the inspiration for this book. The many recovering charismatics who attend there showed me that charismatic gifts can operate in a healthy way—in a Presbyterian church! My six years serving you as a pastor were a wild ride that I will never forget.

To The Neighborhood Church: although we're just starting to live life together, I can't wait to see what God will do in us and through us in the coming years.

I'm also privileged to participate in a small group community that lives life together. You're an extension of my flesh-and-blood family. Thank you for being a part of my life.

Other people I must recognize: Tom Freiling, who began as my roommate and eventually gave me my start in writing. Jeff Braun and Tim Peterson at Bethany House. Also, my agent, Greg

Johnson. My focus group: Anne Thompson, Paul Myskiw, Lori Aguiar, Joel and Lisa Schalla, Stephanie Acosta, Reuben Acosta, James Klassen, Harriet Klassen, and Kelley Klassen. My writers group: Karen Linamen (you are the hostess with the mostest), Beth Lueders, Laura Lisle, Andy Sloan (my driving buddy), Blythe Daniel, and John Perrodin. I'll never forget spending an evening running various ideas through the Sloganizer as we brainstormed titles for this book. What an absolute hoot! Your encouragement, laughter, and creativity kept me going.

Last of all, I must give all glory to God, from whom all blessings flow. "For from him and through him and to him are all things. To him be the glory forever! Amen" (Romans 11:36).

Contents

A Critic and an Apologist

"So . . . what did *you* think of your experience as a charismatic?"

Every time I'm asked that question I cringe. How do I respond to something that stirs up strong, ambivalent emotions of both affection and revulsion? How do I respond to the feeling of buying into a bunch of hooey, yet knowing that elements of truth were woven into the fabric of my experience?

Reflecting on my participation in the charismatic movement unleashes a flood of often contradictory feelings. Pain. Embarrassment. Gratitude.

It's kind of like the way I got along with my younger sister, Lisa, when we were kids. We could fight like cats and dogs and say really mean things to each other. But when a boy at school started picking on her (she was seven and I was fourteen), I couldn't wait to meet him after school:

"If you so much as lay a finger on my little sister, I'll throw you in a trash can and roll you down the street," I scolded the boy in a stern voice. Obviously, the hapless kid was no match for an eighth-grader.

Even today, Lisa and I can spend an evening criticizing our common experience in the charismatic movement. And we have. But if an "outsider" so much as lays a finger on our experience, we're both ready to throw the person in a trash can and roll him down the street. Of course, I mean that in a figurative sense, but in a literal sense, you'd have a catfight on your hands.

Lisa and I are admittedly critics *and* apologists. How can that be?

After leaving the independent charismatic movement, I served as a pastor in a fairly stodgy denomination. Officials loved to parade me around as the wayward Christian gone good. I was presented before groups of impressionable young people to warn them of the evils of the independent charismatic movement. And although I agreed with everything I said, something inside told me I was a traitor. I had left the movement, yet I still believed—deeply—in the fundamental truths that undergird it.

Like a pendulum, I started at the extreme end and allowed the gravitational pull of hurts, disappointments, frustrations, and more embarrassment than I care to admit to propel me to the other side. Yet the opposite end offered me as little rest as my starting point. Pendulums tend to do that. Criticism, negativity, and its bitter offspring, cynicism, never satisfy. So the pendulum returns to its starting point only to offer more disappointment, frustration, and embarrassment.

But eventually the pendulum must come to rest. That's what this book is about: finding a resting place within the charismatic movement. If you're on the opposite end of the swing, you probably understand the insanity, and you just want to get off. If you're actively involved in the charismatic movement, you may still be riding the upswing. Watch out—because whatever goes up must come down. Then again, you may consider yourself a window shopper who's intrigued by what you see in the charismatic movement, but you're hesitant to take the wild ride.

Regardless of your persuasion, my prayer is that this book will help you make peace with the strengths and weaknesses associated with one of the greatest—if not *the* greatest—moves of God in the history of the church.

A Strange and Mysterious Fire

Fire plays a strange and mysterious role in the drama of Scripture. It makes its first appearance as a mysterious firepot and flaming torch when God establishes his covenant with Abram in Genesis 15. In its second appearance, in Genesis 19, fire and sulfur rain down on Sodom and Gomorrah, effectively destroying the cities and creating a gigantic mess . . . with a cesspool we now call the Dead Sea.

Later, in Exodus 3, Moses encountered a burning bush. Strangely enough, the fire never consumed the shrub representing God's presence.

Over three thousand years before Benjamin Franklin invented the fire department, fire symbolized danger and the near impossibility of controlling it. Failing to handle it properly resulted in getting burned, or worse.

While the Israelites wandered in the wilderness, Aaron's sons Nadab and Abihu learned a deadly lesson about fire (you can read about it in Leviticus 10). As they served in the tabernacle, we read that Nadab and Abihu offered "strange fire" (KJV) to the Lord. Other versions of the Bible (like the NIV) translate it "unauthorized fire," some with an asterisk leading you to the literal meaning: "strange fire."

Scholars speculate on the nature of the boys' faux pas. Some say they didn't observe the ritual cleansing rites before entering the tabernacle. Others speculate that the boys copied some kind of practice that the surrounding nations used in worship.

But as is often the case, God left the details of the story in ambiguity. We can't be sure if the boys did it on purpose or just messed up. *Strange.*

Fast-forward fifteen hundred years, and we witness another performance featuring strange fire. On Pentecost Sunday, a fledgling group of Jesus' followers were praying in the Upper Room when suddenly the Holy Spirit entered the stage in all his glory. As his presence was poured out, tongues of holy fire appeared and rested on the believers.

What happened next? If you come from a charismatic background, you could tell this story in your sleep. They all spoke in tongues (we'll delve more into that topic in chapter 2).

How did the people walking the streets of Jerusalem respond? Initially, they were amazed and perplexed. But then they mocked those early Pentecostals, saying, "You're drunk with new wine." (Perhaps Pentecostals weren't known back then for being teetotalers!) *Strange fire.*

Three years earlier, as Jesus' ministry began, John the Baptist described the fate of all chaff: "His winnowing fork is in his hand, and he will clear his threshing floor, gathering his wheat into the barn and burning up the chaff with unquenchable fire" (Matthew 3:12).

In Jesus' day, bread served as a staple in the Middle-Eastern diet. Wheat was the main ingredient, but before it could be ground into flour, the outer husk (or chaff) needed to be removed. The farmer didn't worry about separating the two—he simply tossed the harvested wheat into the air and the wind carried the chaff away.

According to this passage, wheat is good and chaff is bad. Yet during the harvest, they appear as a two-part song-and-dance team. If you want the wheat, you're going to have to tolerate the chaff—at least for a while. But at the right time, in God's time, the wheat is separated from the chaff. And what do you do with chaff? You burn it. In the fire.

Part and parcel to every move of God throughout the ages is wheat and chaff. Spirit and flesh. You can tolerate it for a while, but eventually the time comes for the chaff to be burned. And what does the inferno look like? Strange fire. It's strange because it looks like you're burning the wheat when you're actually burning the chaff.

At the same time, the fire is a holy fire, because it is consuming the impurities, leaving the wheat whole.

In Scripture, fire can represent God's judgment, but it can also represent the purifying work of the Holy Spirit. Strangely enough, it's the same fire. A holy fire.

This book is about wheat and chaff, spirit and flesh, the strange fire and holy fire that judges and purifies. It's also about the strange fire we sometimes offer to God that doesn't quite hit the mark. And if we can be honest, all of us have a little Nadab and Abihu in us that opts for worshiping God on our terms rather than his.

A Word About Recovering Charismatics

Periodically as you read, you will come across the term *recovering charismatic*. If you're a charismatic on the "upswing" of the pendulum, or simply a Holy Spirit seeker, you may be wondering, What does he mean by a recovering charismatic?

While recovery programs are valid and quite helpful, this isn't a study on twelve-step programs. However, I'd like to borrow a few ideas from the recovery movement that pertain to this book:

1. The recovery movement is rooted in the acknowledgment of brokenness.

A woman can't overcome her addiction to Twizzlers until she acknowledges that every day she craves the twisty, shiny, red licorice. The same applies to alcohol, sex, or reruns of *SpongeBob Squarepants* (one of my vices).

A recovering charismatic admits that a line has been crossed, a wound has been inflicted, a conscience has been offended, or a bunch of hooey has been believed. Not only is this so, but now you regret it. Deeply.

Anger characterizes my initial feelings when I reflect on my experience. But since anger is a secondary emotion, something lies far deeper. What is it? I'm still figuring it out, but I think it's pain. The pain of doing some pretty wacky things in the name of the Holy Spirit. The pain of buying into a brand of Christianity that is distinctly Western. The pain of realizing how fallible I really am.

2. The vices that drive us into recovery are inherently good.

Everything is created by God to be enjoyed within the context of his divine plan. The apostle Paul wrote, "All things are yours, whether Paul or Apollos or Cephas or the world or life or death or the present or the future—all are yours, and you are of Christ, and Christ is of God" (1 Corinthians 3:21–23).

Did you notice that word *all*? Do you know what *all* means in the Greek? All means "all." Alcohol isn't inherently evil and neither is sex (whew!). But they can place us in a position where we allow them to master us or take advantage of us and as a result, inflict pain.

The charismatic movement has proven itself to be inherently good: lives changed, people healed, the church empowered in new ways—undoubtedly a sovereign move of God. But somewhere along the way, miraculous gifts and the emphasis on power all too often became the main thing.

Many carnivals and amusement parks incorporate a booth where an artist draws caricatures of people who pass by. The drawing exaggerates a person's distinctive features, which may include a big nose (think Jimmy Durante), a prominent chin (Jay Leno), or poofy hair (Don King).

In a caricature, the peripheral thing becomes the main thing. The "charismatic" gifts, especially speaking in tongues, become the measure of spirituality. And where do caricatures belong?

At carnivals and amusement parks. I fear at times our churches resemble those places, as well.

3. Recovery is more a journey than a destination.

People in recovery acknowledge that their journeys never come to an end. Because of this, we never see ourselves as completely "over" our experiences.

I grew up a charismatic, and I'll always carry that experience with me. At times those feelings of affection and gratitude degenerate into revulsion, pain, and embarrassment.

In my thirty-plus years of involvement in the charismatic movement, I've met people who wanted very badly to speak in tongues, but for some reason, they couldn't or didn't. Others struggled with chronic illnesses and pleaded with God to be healed, but he didn't answer their requests—at least not in this life. These folks remained in their churches, but were relegated to a lower caste—fit for those who weren't spiritual enough or didn't have enough faith.

My malady? I won't let you in on it just yet, but you'll probably figure it out as you read on. My point is this: I don't want to stay in the revulsion, pain, and embarrassment. And if you're a recovering charismatic, or on the verge of becoming one, you probably don't either. We want to get better. We want healing and wholeness.

We're all in different stages of recovery from our shortcomings and flesh (affectionately called our sinful nature), but hopefully this book will give you an opportunity to move on.

Your experience may be similar to mine. You may have been severely hurt by people in this movement, or its theology, and now you're ready to find meaning in it.

Then again, you may be that window shopper who simply wants to make heads or tails of this strange, intriguing yet alluring movement. (You may even be attending an independent charismatic church, and you're trying to get a sense of what's legitimate and what's not.) (I use parentheses because using them is like talking in a whisper . . . so no one at church will hear!)

Regardless of your reason for choosing this book, I invite you to join me as we journey on this path together. At the risk of over-spiritualizing, I'd like you to see this as a pilgrimage. A journey of spiritual significance. On a roller coaster.

Along the way we'll stop at the highs and lows of various charismatic signposts: tongues, healing, television evangelists, authority, "the Word." Hopefully our time together will give you an opportunity to reflect and to find healing and a redemptive sense of significance from your experience.

If you attend a charismatic church, I hope this book helps you separate the wheat from the chaff so you can live more authentically in the power of the Holy Spirit—and still remain in your church.

If you're a Holy Spirit seeker, I hope this book makes you thirstier for more of his work in your life. Paul encouraged us to "earnestly desire the spiritual gifts" (1 Corinthians 14:1 ESV). The spiritual gifts practiced in charismatic churches—including the controversial gifts—are legitimate and important. Unfortunately, they can be abused and confused with hype, flesh, and misunderstanding. May this book help you navigate your way through the ambiguity.

Please understand that my goal is honesty, not criticism. And since no one can claim to be objective, I won't.

You may even have stories or insights you'd like to share. I don't have it all figured out, so I welcome your interaction at *www.strangefireholyfire.com*.

Are you ready to begin the pilgrimage?

CHAPTER 1

So What Is a Charismatic?

Defining Your Terms

Do you want the biblical definition of *charismatic* or the Western, twentieth-century definition?

For two summers in high school I played my violin with a traveling Christian music group called the Continental Singers. One night on the road, I was talking with one of my bandmates and I asked him the charismatic "qualifying question."

"Andy, are you Spirit-filled?"

"Yes."

I excitedly shared with him my charismatic testimony, switching into charismatic insider language and talking about how I received my prayer language and who else in our group was "in" (meaning they spoke in tongues) and who was "out" (they didn't). Then he replied with a chilling answer that stopped me in my tracks.

"It all depends on how you define Spirit-filled. If you mean, 'Do I speak in tongues?' then I guess I'm not. But if you believe, like I do, that every Christian receives the Holy Spirit at salvation, and you're asking if I have the Holy Spirit, then I guess I am."

Oops. Maybe Andy wasn't as "in" as I thought.

"Never mind."

You see, Andy was operating from the biblical definition, and I was operating from the Western, twentieth-century definition.

As a young, naïve, and impressionable product of the charismatic movement, I assumed every Christian understood what "Spirit-filled" meant. "Spirit-filled" churches were filled with "Spirit-filled" people—people who spoke in tongues fluently. "Spirit-filled" was simply another way of saying "charismatic."

Although we abhorred the idea of belonging to a denomination, we did belong to a loose consortium of independent charismatic churches. Attending a non-charismatic church was a no-no unless we were there for a wedding or a funeral.

Occasionally we ventured into other charismatic churches in the area to hear a well-known guest speaker or to imbibe in whatever the Spirit was pouring out in that church. If we really liked the other church and God gave us a release, we might even end up staying there. But all of us knew which churches were okay to attend. They were the ones that believed in "the gifts" (see chapter 3).

"The gifts" rarely meant such common spiritual gifts as encouragement or service. "The gifts" were the spiritual gifts that made many of the other churches feel uncomfortable: tongues, interpretation of tongues, healing, miracles, word of knowledge, and prophecy.

All Christians Are Charismatics (or Is It Pneumatikotics?)

The Greek New Testament uses two different words for spiritual gifts. The first word, *pneumatikos*, can be translated "pertaining to the Spirit" or "spiritual enablement." That's the word the apostle Paul used when he wrote, "Now about *spiritual gifts*, brothers, I do not want you to be ignorant" (1 Corinthians 12:1, italics added).

Interestingly enough, pneumatikos can also be translated "spiritual person." For example, "The *spiritual person* judges all things, but is himself to be judged by no one" (1 Corinthians 2:15 ESV, italics added). Derivatives of this word appear twenty-six times in the New Testament.

The other Greek word—much more common among charismatics than pneumatikos—is *charisma*. Obviously, that word has become the namesake of the movement we know and (sometimes) love. Interestingly enough, it appears seventeen times in the Greek New Testament, nine times fewer than its counterpart.

Unlike pneumatikos, *charisma* never appears in reference to a person or a church. In the interest of precision and being biblical, charismatics should refer to themselves as "pneumatikotics," since the word means "spiritual person." Perhaps our forebears chose the word *charismatic* because it slides off the tongue easier than *pneumatikotic*. That or the fact that the other word sounds too much like *neurotic* (maybe our forebears chose the wrong name)!

Literally translated, *charisma* means "grace gift." In the book of Romans, Paul uses the word in reference to the greatest grace gift of all: salvation (see Romans 6:23). But not once is the word translated as "one who speaks in tongues." Instead, it refers to the smorgasbord of spiritual gifts mentioned in Romans 12; 1 Corinthians 12–14; and 1 Peter 4:10–11.

So maybe Andy was right. In fact, if you believe in any of the spiritual gifts—whether it's tongues and healing or service and administration—you should consider yourself a charismatic. (Try that one on your dispensational friends and watch them squirm!)

Despite the presence of the word in the New Testament, we find no evidence that anyone in the Bible called themselves charismatics or Pentecostals. They simply called themselves Christians, which means "followers of Christ."

> For a whole year Barnabas and Saul met with the church and
> taught great numbers of people. The disciples were called
> Christians first at Antioch.
>
> ACTS 11:26

The Western, Twentieth-Century Definition

In a recent *Christianity Today* article, Grant McClung reported that as of 2006, over 580 million people in the world consider themselves adherents of this global movement. Every year, the number of adherents increases by 19 million, or more than 54,000 people a day! This includes Pentecostals and charismatics (more on their differences in a moment). McClung reports, "At the current rate of growth, some researchers predict there will be one billion Pentecostals by 2025, most located in Asia, Africa, and Latin America."[1]

And which country includes the greatest number? Surprisingly enough, it's not the United States. As of 2002, Brazil claimed a whopping 80 million Pentecostals! Coming in second was the United States at 75 million—but it's the only Western country ranked in the top ten.[2]

For this reason, C. Peter Wagner has commented that the growth of the Pentecostal/charismatic movement, since 1901, "represents what would undoubtedly prove to be one of the highest if not *the* highest recorded rate of growth of a nonpolitical, nonmilitaristic human movement across history."

Makes you feel pretty good, doesn't it?

You Can Smell the Difference Among the Three

Outsiders have a hard time distinguishing among Pentecostals, charismatics, and what some call "third wave-rs." But insiders can smell the difference from a distance.

For the most part, Pentecostals find their roots in the Holiness movements of the late 1800s. Interestingly enough, that makes first cousins out of Pentecostals, Nazarenes, and to a lesser extent, Methodists. And in many ways their teachings are very similar.

In fact, close your eyes sometime and listen to a Pentecostal and a Nazarene talk. You won't be able to tell the difference as they wax eloquent about camp meetings, revivals, and a second blessing. My definition of a Nazarene is a Pentecostal who doesn't speak in tongues.

Pentecostals trace their beginnings back to the early 1900s in Topeka, Kansas. Charles Parham used his Bethel Bible College as a platform to teach his students, and later the world, about the baptism of the Holy Spirit with the evidence of speaking in tongues. Although he initially didn't speak in tongues, he believed its manifestation was right around the corner. And it was.

Pentecostalism was forged in the fires of revivalism, which explains their emphasis on personal conversion, holiness, and the sanctification of the believer. They also believe that after conversion a person can and should pursue a "second work of grace," much like the Methodists and Nazarenes. Pentecostals call this the baptism of the Holy Spirit with the evidence of speaking in tongues. To the Pentecostal, the baptism of the Holy Spirit and speaking in tongues are essentially the same thing.

Pentecostal denominations include the Assemblies of God, Church of God (Cleveland, Tennessee), International Church of the Foursquare Gospel, and the Church of God in Christ.

The second distinctive movement of the Holy Spirit in America during the twentieth century finds its genesis in the charismatic renewal of the 1960s. Dennis Bennett, an Episcopalian rector in Van Nuys, California, is credited with starting this movement when he announced to his congregation that he had been baptized in the Holy Spirit and spoke in tongues. Bennett later penned two extremely influential books: *Nine O'Clock in the Morning* and *The Holy Spirit and You.*

Rather than leave the denomination, he sought to remain in the Episcopal Church. Quickly thereafter, the charismatic renewal spread to other Protestant denominations and gained a strong foothold in the Roman Catholic Church.

The charismatic renewal exists in practically every denomination, ranging from the Disciples of Christ to the Southern Baptists (seriously!). Although beneficiaries of this movement believe in the widest understanding of the expression of the spiritual gifts—from administration to tongues—the rest of their theology more or less reflects the distinctives of their particular denomination.

Third wave-rs are a little harder to define because they share similarities with people in the Pentecostal and charismatic renewal movements yet differ enough to be included in a separate category.

Churches of this kind can range from "independent" churches to Vineyard churches. Many of these people began in renewal movements within the mainline denominations, but because they weren't well-received, they were subsequently forced into organizing congregations of their own. Scholarly types refer to them as "neocharismatics," but I've never heard pastors or laypeople refer to themselves by that designation. It fits like an old sweater from days (and sizes) gone by. If you were to ask people in "neocharismatic" churches what they call themselves, they would simply reply, "charismatic."

Because the vast majority of charismatic churches operate independently of one another, or any denomination, their distinctive beliefs are a little harder to pin down. Generally, they believe in the gifts of the Spirit like Pentecostals do, but their views of the relationship between tongues and the baptism of the Holy Spirit vary as much as their churches.

The International Dictionary of Pentecostal and Charismatic Movements breaks down the three groups in the English-speaking Western world as follows (2002):

	Pentecostal	Charismatic Renewal	Charismatic
United States	4,946,390	19,473,158	50,736,451
Canada	504,551	2,596,361	1,324,088
United Kingdom (England, Ireland, Scotland, and Wales)	280,184	4,556,774	1,473,042
Total	**5,731,125**	**26,626,293**	**53,533,581**

In the United States, twice as many people worship in charismatic churches than in the other two groups combined. On the other hand, nearly twice as many people in Canada and the United Kingdom are products of the charismatic renewal within the denominations than of the other two combined.

All told, over 53 million people in the U.S., Canada, and the United Kingdom could be considered charismatics. That's nearly the population of California and New York put together. Charismatics in the United States alone outnumber the entire population of England! Incredibly enough, over 85 million people consider themselves adherents to one of the three groups.

Because my experience lies primarily among charismatics, this book focuses on a large subset within that group, which I refer to as the Independent Charismatic Movement (not to be confused with the charismatic renewal within the historically non-charismatic denominations). These churches operate independently or within a loose configuration of networks, but they are *not* a member of a denomination. Perish the thought!

From this point on, that's what I mean when I refer to a charismatic church or an independent charismatic church. From my experience, churches of this sort operate from the Western, twentieth-century definition. Since people who attend these churches call themselves charismatics, I'll do the same.

For a while, I considered the term *post-charismatic* as my preferred label for people like me, who had emerged from the movement a little tattered, battered, and torn. But after a Web search on *post-charismatic*, I discovered that the vast number of results referred to a movement within Hare Krishna.

Why couldn't the Hare Krishnas choose *Krishnamatic* instead?

We won't be opening that can of worms.

CHAPTER 2

Everyone Repeat After Me

The Importance of Tongues

Recently I gathered a dozen people in my home to share our varied experiences in the independent charismatic movement. Some were active participants and others were recovering charismatics.

I began our evening by asking the group a very general question: "How did God use your participation in the charismatic movement to positively affect your life?"

Immediately Reuben's hand waved in the air. "How are you defining a 'charismatic'?"

"We'll get to that in a minute," I replied. Because I didn't want to influence their initial responses, I purposely avoided placing any parameters on their experience.

One by one, the people in my living room reflected on how God had positively affected their lives through what we all acknowledged was a sovereign move of the Holy Spirit.

"I felt forgiven."

"Scripture came alive."

"The academic became experiential."

"I fell in love with Jesus."

Reuben looked at me again. He wanted answers.

"In just a little bit, Reuben." The sweet presence of the Holy Spirit seemed to permeate the room as we recounted landmark spiritual events that shaped our lives.

Finally, as our preliminary discussion concluded, I asked the group, "How did your churches define a charismatic?"

"Tongues," they answered in unison—including Reuben.

If you've participated in the charismatic movement, no definition is necessary.

Tongues is *the* litmus test, the dividing line, of what defines a charismatic in our culture as well as the movement behind it. Oddly enough, though, no one in the group that met in my living room offered a positive memory about tongues. Their experience with tongues wasn't necessarily negative, but the movement encompassed something so much bigger than one spiritual gift.

Passing the Litmus Test

My induction into the charismatic movement began rather innocuously. When I was seven years old, a pastor visited my Sunday school class and asked if anyone wanted to receive the "baptism of the Holy Spirit with the evidence of speaking in tongues." It's a mouthful to say all at once, especially to a group of children, but that's an important phrase in the charismatic lexicon—something you have to understand before you can become a card-carrying member. Besides, our teachers had done a pretty good job, because most of us kids understood what he was talking about.

After a very brief explanation, a handful of us stepped into the middle of a circle, the pastor laid hands on us, and I spoke in tongues. No fireworks. No tears. No drama. For me, the experience was rather unemotional.

After church, my family got in the car and drove home. As we were driving, we practiced the weekly Sunday afternoon ritual performed in automobiles across the country: "What did you learn at church today?" one of my parents asked. My older sister, Lori, answered first, and then it was my turn. I gave a one- or two-sentence answer about whatever Bible story we studied that day. And then, more as an afterthought, I mentioned, "Oh yeah, Pastor Lloyd prayed for me and I spoke in tongues." My parents didn't say anything, but after we got home, while Mom put the finishing touches on the pot roast, Dad said he wanted to pray with me. I think he was just checking me out!

Apparently I passed the test because after we prayed together for just a few short moments, my dad grinned at me and said, "Let's eat dinner."

I was in!

Tongues was, and is, a very helpful gift that has enabled me to pray about situations when I didn't know what to pray. It has served as a weapon in spiritual warfare and has given me insight into God's ways. And it has definitely cultivated a deeper, more intimate walk with Christ.

Maintaining the (Dis)Unity of the Spirit

While still in elementary school, I picked up the belief that people who spoke in tongues were set apart. Special. I had something that other believers, even seemingly more mature believers, needed in order to become better Christians.

"Speaking in tongues is like riding a ten-speed bike," I often explained. "In second gear you can only go so fast, but you can go a lot faster in tenth gear. If Billy Graham spoke in tongues he would be an even more effective evangelist." To be honest, it felt good knowing I had something Billy needed.

My friend Dave, a committed follower of Jesus who doesn't claim to be a charismatic, was once told he wouldn't go to heaven if he didn't speak in tongues. Speaking in tongues, apparently, wasn't even the initial evidence of the baptism of the Holy Spirit;

it was the initial evidence of being saved. Does that make him a lesser Christian than me?

In my experience, pastors never lined up the higher caste charismatics on one side of the room so they could take potshots at the lower caste charismatics. In order to teach a class, prospective teachers were never asked to speak in tongues in front of a pastor or elder to prove they were spiritual enough to teach others.

The dividing line was much more subtle. Unless a person exercised the gift of tongues in public, or somebody prayed in tongues out loud during a prayer service, no one knew who was a Holy Spirit "have" and who was a Holy Spirit "have-not." And few people with any social graces ventured to ask.

We prayed for people to receive their prayer language. If they didn't speak, we figured they either had unconfessed sin in their lives or were afraid to speak out. If they just spoke out, they would be given the language of the Spirit . . . like every Christian.

We listened to charismatic speakers and read books written by charismatic authors—men and women with something to say, who also spoke in tongues. We valued their words more than your "run of the mill" Christian speakers and authors because their eyes had been opened to the ways of the Spirit.

We subscribed to newsletters and magazines that extolled the glories of the Holy Spirit at work in our churches (often called "revivals"). But more times than not, the underlying reason why we were attracted to the stories, articles, and columns was because the writers and the articles passed the litmus test. They were written by people who spoke in tongues about other people who spoke in tongues. From our perspective (mine included), the gift of tongues opened the way to special revelation knowledge that outsiders would never understand.

Most ironic is that the Holy Spirit's purpose in distributing gifts (which includes tongues) is to build unity in the church. Paul encouraged the Ephesians to "make every effort to keep the unity of the Spirit through the bond of peace" (Ephesians 4:3). Yet all too often this particular gift of the Spirit has been perverted, conflicting with the Holy Spirit's purpose.

Most damaging of all, however, are the countless stories of people who desperately wanted more of the Holy Spirit, who believed that tongues was the magic pill that would solve all of their problems, and felt subtly marginalized at church because they never received their prayer language. A lifetime living as the overlooked charismatic stepchild would condition anyone into believing, *There must be something wrong with me.*

If you're one of those people, please read closely: YOU ARE NOT GOD'S STEPCHILD—YOU ARE A CHILD OF GOD.

"Yet to all who received him"—that's Jesus—"to those who believed in his name, he gave the right to become children of God" (John 1:12). The reason you didn't receive the gift of tongues isn't because you have unconfessed sin or you're riddled with fear or you lack enough faith or you aren't desperate enough for God. We all have unconfessed sin, we all struggle with fear from time to time, none of us live by faith as we should, and we all fail to realize the depth of our need for God.

Tongues: A Gift, Not *the* Gift

Every charismatic pastor worth his weight in gold dust knows that the way to build a Sunday school program . . . oops, I mean ministry (using the word *program* is the kiss of death!), is to teach a class on the book of First Corinthians. Most amazing to me regarding this phenomenon is that First Corinthians is the favorite book of Pentecostals and charismatics, and yet one of the primary points Paul makes in his letter is that we should avoid making tongues the point!

> Are all apostles? Are all prophets? Are all teachers? Do all work miracles? Do all have gifts of healing? Do all speak in tongues?

Do all interpret? But eagerly desire the greater gifts. And now I
will show you the most excellent way.

1 CORINTHIANS 12:29–31

The church in Corinth was a mess. Divisions were forming
over the authority of various teachers. With the church's blessing,
a man was living in immorality with his father's wife. Their worship gatherings were a tongues-saturated, charismatic free-for-all.
Sound eerily familiar?

Paul then asks seven rhetorical questions. Are all apostles?
prophets? teachers? Do all work miracles, possess gifts of healing, speak in tongues, or interpret tongues? The obvious answer
is no.

Then he exhorts them to "eagerly desire the greater gifts." What
are the greater gifts? Paul doesn't give a definitive list, but he does
point to one in particular—prophecy (see 1 Corinthians 14:1).
Then he explains, "Everyone who prophesies speaks to men for
their strengthening, encouragement and comfort. He who speaks
in a tongue edifies himself, but he who prophesies edifies the
church. I would like every one of you to speak in tongues, but I
would rather have you prophesy" (1 Corinthians 14:3–5). Tongues
are good, Paul seems to say, but prophecy is better.

If anything, charismatics should make prophecy the point, since
it's the greater gift. But they don't. Why? Because they know that
not everyone has the gift of prophecy.

More important than prophecy or tongues, the more excellent
way is love. Why do you think Paul sandwiched 1 Corinthians
13—the love chapter—right in the middle of his discussion on
spiritual gifts? Chances are the church in Corinth shared a similar
struggle to many churches today.

I don't doubt the sincerity of the many charismatics who inad-
vertently split churches and create divisions in their congregations
over tongues. But I can't help asking, "Did the people on the other
end feel loved?" If the answer is no, then many of their efforts

amounted to no more than a noisy gong or a clanging cymbal (see 1 Corinthians 13:1 NASB).

Is It a Spiritual Gift or a Personal Prayer Language?

This brings us to the all-important question: Is the gift of tongues used in a public setting different from a personal prayer language?

The charismatics I have known usually reply yes—but base their answer on experience rather than Scripture. Like me, many charismatics pray in tongues but have never felt moved by the Holy Spirit to exercise their gift of tongues in a public setting.

But what does Scripture say?

Only Luke (the author of Acts) and Paul make a point of discussing the subject of tongues. It shouldn't be overlooked that they were also partners in ministry. However, none of the other writers of the New Testament directly mention tongues. Of the firsthand witnesses to Pentecost—John, Peter, and possibly James (the brother of Jesus, not one of the twelve disciples)—not one mentions the gift even once! Peter even discusses spiritual gifts in 1 Peter 4:10–11, but somehow overlooks including it in his list. Ironically enough, he begins the list with prophecy (speaking the "oracles of God" ESV).

Of the thirty-one times Luke or Paul use the word *tongues*, the majority of references refer to "speaking" in tongues (eighteen times). "Praying in tongues" is only mentioned in one passage.

> For if I pray in a tongue, my spirit prays, but my mind is unfruitful. So what shall I do? I will pray with my spirit, but I will also pray with my mind; I will sing with my spirit, but I will also sing with my mind.
>
> *1 CORINTHIANS 14:14–15*

Paul acknowledged that he spoke in tongues, but he minimized it. "I thank God that I speak in tongues more than all of you," he explained. "But in the church I would rather speak five intelligible words to instruct others than ten thousand words in a tongue" (1 Corinthians 14:18–19).

So is there a difference between the two? I don't know. Scripture isn't clear about it, and the firsthand witnesses to Pentecost refused to make it a point in their writings. Perhaps we should follow their lead and refuse to make it the point, as well. For this reason, I wouldn't build a church on its use, nor would I want to define a movement by it.

With all the controversy surrounding tongues, and the haziness in Scripture regarding its use, should we avoid it?

Not at all.

Tongues is one of many spiritual gifts. If you have it, be thankful for it and speak it frequently. If you don't have it, seek it, like Paul says in 1 Corinthians 14. But more than that, earnestly desire that God would speak through you in words everyone can understand.

If you've been wounded because you never spoke in tongues, please understand that the people who hurt you probably did so not because they didn't care but because they did. Perhaps God has something else just as precious for you. If churches in New Testament times struggled over the use of tongues, why should it be any different today?

If you've wounded others because you thought they weren't "spiritual" enough to speak in tongues, own your sin. Confess it to God, and then find the people you've wounded and ask for their forgiveness.

Most important, don't let tongues become an idol. Tongues aren't the point—Jesus is—so don't sweat it.

CHAPTER 3

Us vs. Them

Spiritual Pride and Our Perception of Non-Charismatics

After John Wimber became a Christian, he began reading his Bible. Actually, he didn't just read his Bible, he consumed it. Page after page, he observed a lifestyle that he longed for, a life that differed from anything he had seen.

Weeks later, after attending yet another boring church service, he asked one of the church layleaders, "When do we get to do the stuff?"

"What stuff?" the leader asked.

"You know, the stuff here in the Bible," John replied. "You know, like stuff Jesus did—raising people from the dead, healing the blind and the paralyzed. You know, that stuff."

"Well, we don't do that anymore."

"You don't? Then what *do* you do?"

"What we did this morning."

Incredulous, John asked, "For that I gave up drugs?"

Because they didn't make room for "the stuff," John Wimber

left that church and eventually helped start what became known as the Vineyard churches.

Doing the Stuff When Others Don't

Swimming in the mainstream of the charismatic movement can be exhilarating. When you witness the Holy Spirit at work, you rarely question his ability or existence. You know he's real because you've seen him doing "the stuff."

But how do you respond when you attend a church that does the stuff and your friends attend churches that don't?

You: "Hey, Frank. How was your weekend?"

Frank: "It was okay. My mother-in-law's lumbago was giving her fits, so we spent Saturday at her house cleaning up after her twelve cats. We vacuumed so much cat hair out of her drapes that we're planning to use it to knit her a sweater for Christmas. How was your weekend?"

You: "Great! We went to Johnny's football game on Saturday. He sprained his ankle pretty bad, so we prayed for him at church on Sunday and he got healed. Praise God! By the way, how was church for you?"

Frank: "You know, the choir sang. Pastor Ted preached an inspiring message, then we went home. Same old, same old."

Charismatics aren't satisfied listening to *inspiring* messages. At church, they want *anointed* messages. The "same old, same old" simply isn't good enough when you've experienced "the stuff."

But are churches that do the stuff better than churches that don't?

When your church does stuff that other churches don't—exciting stuff, no less—you want to share what you have with your friends, and you want your friends' churches to be like yours. And why wouldn't you? They're missing out!

Before long, your authentic concern metamorphoses into spiritual pride.

As a child, I was exposed to some pretty dramatic miracles and healings. If I had my way, I would have hung a banner in front of my church that read, "Redeemer Temple: the church Jesus would attend . . . if he were still around!"

Of course, if Jesus attends my church, what does that imply about all the other churches?

It's Not Pride. I Just Know That I Know That I Know!

Quick quiz. Have you ever:

- Insisted on only reading books written by authors who speak in tongues?
- Believed that your non-charismatic friends would be better Christians if they were charismatic like you?
- Assumed anything significant happening in a church must come from a charismatic church?
- Jokingly referred to non-charismatic churches as "God's frozen chosen"?
- Believed that your job is to bring the Holy Spirit to other people and churches?

If so, then welcome to the club!

Many of us charismatics looked (or still look) down on non-charismatics. We believed in *all* the spiritual gifts—including tongues and healing. We didn't just talk about doing the stuff, we did it. And God's hand was obviously on us because he worked so powerfully through us. Besides, our churches were growing while many of theirs weren't. At least, that's what we thought.

But many non-charismatics looked down on us because we weren't dignified, educated, or "balanced" (don't you hate that word?) . . . all we wanted to do was speak in tongues! We acted strange and believed every "fresh word" that came down the pike. Not to mention, we were just so emotional.

Like our predecessors, the Pentecostals, we encountered criticism from other churches for our sometimes odd behavior and were subject to some good old-fashioned misunderstanding. Our low self-esteem and desire for self-protection prompted us to criticize the people who criticized us. Of course, the fact that we did "the stuff" only proved to support our case. As a result, we developed a culture of our own.

Over time, people who only indulge in charismatic influences tend to see reality through a singular charismatic lens. We begin to believe that only charismatics have something significant to say to the church and to the world. We only buy books by people who speak in tongues. We fellowship with people who worship like we do. Besides, we're the fastest growing movement in the world, so God must be on our side.

For a time I attended a charismatic church whose worship team was led by a man who—gasp!—didn't speak in tongues. Incensed, I met with an elder in the church (not with the worship leader, of course!) to ask some hard questions: "How can you trust a man who isn't 'Spirit-filled' to lead the congregation in worship?" I asked.

"We believe that God can use anyone, whether or not they speak in tongues," the gracious man responded.

Despite my critical attitude toward non-charismatics, I took any counter-criticism as a personal attack. In the culture we created, news stories that portrayed any of our leaders in a negative light were viewed as outright attacks from Satan (why didn't God strike those godless journalists with a bolt of lightning?). In retrospect, some news stories were presented with an obvious bias, but others were just reporting the facts.

As a result, we became somewhat "charismacentric." To be ethnocentric means to assume that a particular ethnic group is superior to others. Charismacentric would mean, then, that we believe our charismatic culture and beliefs are superior to others.

Non-charismatic Christians are legitimate, just not as legitimate as we are.

Spiritual pride is as old as the serpent in the garden of Eden. It plagues all of us—charismatic, recovering charismatic, non-charismatic, Holy Spirit seeker, or none of the above. Rather than deny it, we're better off owning it.

The Holy Spirit—a Person or a Commodity?

An underlying reason fueling our pride was our misguided theology. Although we waxed long about the "person of the Holy Spirit," we often treated him more like a commodity.

You know what a commodity is. It's a product that can be traded or sold, like a crate of oranges or a pork belly. People around the world trade commodities at commodities exchanges. Because commodities have no feelings, you can do with them as you wish. When you go to the store and purchase an orange, you can eat it, throw it at a car driving by, or share it with someone. The orange doesn't care because it has no feelings.

Some say, "The problem with all the sickness in the world is that we just don't get enough vitamin C. If everyone ate enough oranges, everything would be fine. What we need in this world is more oranges."

In the same way, I fear we may have treated the Holy Spirit like that orange. At times I've heard charismatics—including myself— say, "The problem with the church today is that they just don't have enough of the Holy Spirit. If some of those churches would just be a little more open, everything would be fine. What we need in the church is more of the Holy Spirit."

Granted, we *do* need more of the ministry of the Holy Spirit in our churches. But all too often we refer to the Holy Spirit as an "it" rather than a "him." If the Holy Spirit is a commodity, then he is something to be obtained. Once he belongs to us, we can do with him whatever we wish: share him with our friends, command him to heal the sick, call on him to find us a parking space, *and bring him to churches that don't have him.*

If we "have" the Holy Spirit, then we control him. By praying in tongues, singing praise and worship choruses, or speaking the Word long enough, we can make him show up.

When we treat the Holy Spirit like a commodity, we draw lines between those who have him and those who don't (according to our definition). Like the Star-Belly Sneetches and the Plain-Belly Sneetches in Dr. Seuss's book *Sneetches Are Sneetches*, what matters is "do they have stars on thars?"

But do we have the Holy Spirit or does he have us? And who controls whom?

> You, however, are controlled not by the sinful nature but by the Spirit, if the Spirit of God lives in you. And if anyone does not have the Spirit of Christ, he does not belong to Christ.
>
> *ROMANS 8:9*

Jesus described the Holy Spirit this way:

> The wind blows wherever it pleases. You hear its sound, but you cannot tell where it comes from or where it is going. So it is with everyone born of the Spirit.
>
> *JOHN 3:8*

It's no mistake that the Greek and Hebrew words for Spirit are translated "wind" or "breath." We can't control the Holy Spirit any more than we can control the wind. If we could control the Holy Spirit, would he still be God? Not the God of the Bible, but rather a god created in our image.

Romans 8:9 also answers the question, "Do all Christians have the Holy Spirit?" with a resounding yes! Either they have the Spirit of Christ and belong to Christ or they don't have the Spirit of Christ and don't belong to Christ. "Spirit of God" and "Spirit of Christ" both refer to the Holy Spirit. No one can have part of the Holy Spirit—it's all or nothing.

The same is true of all churches that confess Jesus Christ as Lord. We can't "bring" the Holy Spirit to churches, because the Holy Spirit is equally at work in both charismatic churches and non-charismatic churches. However, we can help them recognize the Holy Spirit already at work. Let me qualify this statement by admitting that plenty of avowed non-charismatics have also helped me recognize the work of the Holy Spirit in my life.

The Antidote to Spiritual Pride

"Knowledge puffs up," Paul wrote, "but love builds up" (1 Corinthians 8:1). Truth is dangerous—not just because it changes lives but because it so easily affects people in such negative ways. People who gain access into knowledge that others don't have can easily get puffed up with pride because they have something that others don't have, but need.

We shouldn't be surprised by this tendency, because it was modeled for us in the garden. The serpent tempted Adam and Eve by enticing them with special revelation knowledge: "For God knows that when you eat of it your eyes will be opened, and you will be like God, knowing good and evil" (Genesis 3:5). Pride lies at the root of all sin. When we seek to be like God, knowing good and evil, we no longer need him.

Following Adam and Eve's lead, we often seek knowledge that distinguishes us from others. It's knowledge that sets us apart and gives us power over the poor souls who don't know what we know. "Knowledge is power," Sir Francis Bacon once wrote.

Like the gravitational pull of the earth, knowledge frequently gets sucked into pride's ravenous vortex. Whether it applies to auto mechanics, quantum mechanics, or the ways of the Spirit, only one way exists out of its inescapable pull.

Humility.

Have you ever wondered why Paul neglected to include humility as a fruit of the Spirit? He remembered to include love, joy, peace, patience, kindness, goodness, faithfulness, gentleness, and self-control in Galatians 5:22–23, but failed to name the antidote to the root of all sin.

Is Paul guilty of negligence? No.

The fruit of the Spirit is the fruit of the Spirit's work in our lives. We can't force the fruit to manifest itself, it just happens— with the Spirit's help. Like a garden, we provide nutrients and water, but the Spirit produces the fruit.

On the other hand, humility isn't the fruit of the Spirit's work in our lives. Rather, it's an act of the will. "Humble yourselves," both James and Peter exhort us (James 4:10; 1 Peter 5:6). We don't water our spiritual garden to produce humility, we humble ourselves.

Here's how it applies to our experience in the charismatic movement: God's Word is truth (John 17:17). Regardless of our opinions or desires, it never changes. "The grass withers and the flowers fall, but the word of our God stands forever" (Isaiah 40:8).

However, our culture, biases, and experiences color it. Objective truth exists, but let's be honest: we're subjective people.

Humility means understanding that there's always a chance we could be wrong. For this reason, we must treat people who have opposing views or even contradicting experiences with respect.

When we stumble onto something profound, God-breathed, even something that looks like a bona fide outpouring of God's Spirit that could usher in the end of the age, we still must respond in humility, because we could be wrong. We may think we have it right, but there's always an outside chance that the burning fire shut up in our bones is really the chimichanga we ate last night at Pedro's Mexican Café.

Granted, God gives us some guides in our quest for truth: the community of faith (a fancy way of saying the local church); the core historic teachings of the church; his Word; and his Spirit, who guides us into all truth (John 16:13). But we must never claim to have a corner on truth, because truth is too great for any person to master. Besides, God must be pretty small if he can be defined by our conception of him.

In his discussion about knowledge's propensity to puff us up, Paul also explains, "The man who thinks he knows something does not yet know as he ought to know" (1 Corinthians 8:2). The most dangerous people in the world are not the ones who know that they know not—it's the ones who know not that they know not. Avoid them!

It never ceases to amaze me that God entrusts his infallible Word into the hands of his very fallible people—people who know not.

Does a person need to speak in tongues in order to live the Spirit-filled life? I don't think so, but I could be wrong.

Is it always God's desire to heal people when we pray?

Does the gift of "apostle" still exist?

Why did God allow you to be hurt by people you trusted?

We'll look at these questions in the coming chapters, and I'll offer some of my opinions.

But I could be wrong.

CHAPTER 4

Christian History Begins With Agnes Ozman . . . Or Does It?

The Presence of the Gifts Since Pentecost

Charismatics and Pentecostals trace their origins to January 1, 1901—the first day of the twentieth century—when Agnes Ozman became the first person in the modern age to speak in tongues. A student in Charles Parham's Bethel Bible College in Topeka, Kansas, Agnes Ozman, reportedly spoke in Chinese for three days, unable to communicate in English. Frustrated by her inability to converse with her instructor and fellow students, she tried expressing herself in writing, only to scribble in Chinese as well.

Charismatics often treat this event as the beginning of a new move of the Spirit—a move not seen since the New Testament church. They may not know Agnes Ozman's name or the significance of her experience, but the contemporary charismatic leaders I have known only read and quote authors who arrived on the scene after Miss Ozman.

Pentecostal pioneers like Maria Woodworth-Etter and Smith

Wigglesworth taught us about *Signs and Wonders* and *Ever-Increasing Faith*. Early charismatics like Larry Christenson and Dennis and Rita Bennett expounded on *The Christian Family*, and *The Holy Spirit and You*. Later, authors like Jim Cymbala and Joyce Meyer introduced us to *Fresh Wind, Fresh Fire* and *Battlefield of the Mind*.

I See Dead People

When I enrolled at Fuller Seminary as a young, exuberant charismatic, I packed all my treasured books by Bennett, Wigglesworth, and other charismatic leaders—fully prepared to rely on them as primary resources.

Now, you have to understand that to seminarians, size matters—the size of one's theological book collection, of course! If you have in your possession an extensive collection of books written by esteemed theologians, you can immediately command the respect of other, lesser seminarians.

As I moved in, I was greeted by a fellow alum from Oral Roberts University. "I can't wait to see your books!" Chris remarked as we began unpacking our boxes.

I can't wait for you to see them, too, I thought.

A few days later, I stopped by Chris's apartment and asked to see his books. Most of them were written by unfamiliar authors like Teresa of Avila, Brother Lawrence, and Charles Spurgeon. *Poor Chris,* I thought. *He's such a poor seminary student that he can't afford new books like mine.*

Finally the day came for Chris to repay the favor.

"Hey, Mike, can I see your books?"

I welcomed Chris into our apartment and stood back with a smile on my face as he scanned my stash. Dennis Bennett, Smith Wigglesworth, and James Robison welcomed him to my collection.

Awkward silence.

"So, Chris, what do you think?"

"They're okay," Chris replied, his grimace betraying his true feelings. "You know, I'm too busy reading books by dead people to read anything by people who are still alive."

Ouch . . . I think.

History Repeats Itself

Chris had a great point, though. This isn't necessarily an indictment on charismatics, it's an indictment on modern society. At least in the collective American conscience, we assume the only people with something valid to say are people who are still alive. Historically, though, charismatics have treated Agnes Ozman's Pentecostal experience as the second coming of the church—with the Christian "dark ages" spanning over nineteen hundred years (since the end of the New Testament era).

The biblical writers, however, didn't share the same values regarding books written by dead people. In 1 Corinthians 10, Paul warned the church in Corinth against falling into idolatry. By recalling Israel's rebellion in the wilderness over fifteen hundred years earlier, he explained that "these things . . . were written for our instruction" (1 Corinthians 10:11 NASB). In other words, Israel's failings in the wilderness were recorded in the Old Testament so the people in Paul's day, as well as you and I, could learn from their mistakes.

Then, just a few lines later, Paul wrote, "No temptation has overtaken you that is not common to man" (1 Corinthians 10:13 ESV). Looking at the context, Paul seems to be saying that the temptation common to man is the temptation everyone has faced for years, even centuries. He could have just as easily prefaced the passage by saying, "History repeats itself." Our struggles with sin repeat themselves in people around the globe, year after year, century after century.

No matter how excruciating our pain, no matter how

hopeless our struggle or overwhelming the enticement, countless people have faced a similar temptation to give up or give in. "There is nothing new under the sun," Solomon wrote in Ecclesiastes 1:9.

The immortal words of American philosopher George Santayana ring in my head as I ponder this: "Those who cannot learn from history are doomed to repeat it." We desperately need history to avoid repeating our failures of the past. But we also need history to build upon the spiritual foundation of those who have gone before us.

Snapshots of the Holy Spirit at Work

This begs the questions, "Is the charismatic movement something new or a continuation of the Holy Spirit's work over the centuries?" "Do dead people have something to say, or should we focus our spiritual growth primarily on the latest *rhema* word broadcasted over the Christian airwaves?"

The implications of these questions are pretty significant. If the charismatic movement followed all those years of spiritual darkness, then the Trinity must have taken a long vacation (they likely caught the last train to the coast—the Father, Son, and Holy Ghost!), with almost two thousand years of people sentenced to an eternity in hell, or at best, a remnant eking by on a dry, lifeless faith. Would God allow nearly two millennia to pass without a consistent witness comprising more than a remnant of faithful worshipers?

But if the dramatic events of the last one hundred years are a continuation of what God has done over the centuries, well, that changes the way we respond to this great move of the Spirit.

To answer this question, let's take a look at a few snapshots from church history.

Montanists

In AD 155—about a hundred years after Paul wrote 1 Corinthians—a pagan priest from Phrygia (in present-day Turkey), named Montanus, converted to Christianity. Following his conversion, Eusebius, the early-church historian, reported that Montanus "raved, and began to babble and utter strange things, prophesying in a manner contrary to the constant custom of the Church handed down by tradition from the beginning." Montanus declared a new era of the Holy Spirit with new power, prophetic leadership, and a greater commitment to living holy lives.

I'm not making this up—sounds eerily familiar, doesn't it?

Two women joined Montanus, forming a trinity of prophets who proclaimed that their prophecies superseded the authority of Scripture. The Montanists, as they were called, criticized the mainstream church for her laziness and neglect in exercising the spiritual gifts. The church returned the favor by vigorously opposing the Montanists, declaring them heretics.

Philip Schaff, the highly respected nineteenth-century church historian, commented that the church objected to the way in which the prophecies were given and not the prophecies themselves. The church leaders "admitted that the prophecies contained much that was true, but the soberer sense of the Church at large objected decidedly to the frenzied ecstasy in which they were delivered."[1]

The Montanists faced a great deal of criticism, but eventually Tertullian of Carthage, one of the most prominent leaders in the early church, joined their ranks. You may have heard of Tertullian. He coined the phrase "The blood of martyrs is the seed of the church," as well as commonly used Christian terms like Trinity and Old Testament and New Testament. This great leader of the church believed in the legitimacy of tongues as well as other controversial spiritual gifts.

Although it suffered from odd religious practices and unorthodox teachings—the nature of the strange and holy fire—Montanism nevertheless existed within the church as a renewal movement of sorts. And despite the fact that its impact wasn't as far-ranging as the modern charismatic movement, it lasted five hundred years.

Think about that for a moment—a renewal movement that lasted four hundred years (mid-second century to sixth century AD). To give a little context, the Pentecostal/charismatic movement is only a hundred years old. Where will it be in another three hundred years?

Waldensians

Around 1175, Peter Waldo, a wealthy merchant in Lyons, France, experienced a dramatic conversion and decided to follow Christ's example by giving away his worldly goods and leading a simple life of poverty and preaching. He translated the New Testament from Latin into his native tongue and encouraged people to read Scripture for themselves. Soon Waldo gained a sizable following, with men and women imitating his lifestyle of poverty, preaching, and proclamation of the Gospel. Like the followers of St. Francis of Assisi, his contemporary in Italy, they were also committed to meeting the needs of the poor.

Since translating Scripture into the local vernacular and preaching without the authorization of the local clergy were forbidden by the Roman Catholic authorities, the Waldensians faced a great deal of persecution. Eventually they were excommunicated from the mother church. This, however, didn't stop them.

Like the Montanists, they shared a common belief in healing. Note the words of their confession from 1431:

> Therefore concerning the anointing of the sick, we hold it as an article of faith, and profess sincerely from the heart that sick persons, when they ask it, may lawfully be anointed with anointing oil by one who joins them in praying that it may be efficacious to the healing of the body according to the design and end and effect mentioned by the apostles; and we profess

that such an anointing performed according to the apostolic design and practice will be healing and profitable.[2]

As is true of many renewal movements (are we listening?), the Waldensians began claiming they were the "true church." Granted, the persecution enacted by the Roman Catholic authorities explains to a large extent why they drew this conclusion, but claims of spiritual exclusivity lead people—and movements—down dangerous paths.

This group, also known as the Huguenots, experienced continued renewal for three hundred and fifty years, until they joined forces with the Reformers of the sixteenth century. Despite their work at tilling the soil for the Reformation, the movement today exists as a shadow of its former self. Nevertheless, remnants remain eight hundred years after its inception.

Anabaptists

The Anabaptists appeared about the same time as Martin Luther, although they differed from him because they believed, in part, that he didn't take the Reformation far enough. Founded in part by the great reformer Ulrich Zwingli but emboldened by the teachings of Menno Simons, the Anabaptists believed in living their faith, sharing it with others, taking God's Word literally, rejection of infant baptism, the separation of church and state, and pacifism.

One very early Anabaptist leader, a friend of Luther's, started a charismatic fire in Germany that went up in flames. Thomas Müntzer, a former priest steeped in classical education as well as the mystics, began serving a church in the Saxony region of Germany in 1520.

Three men in Müntzer's congregation began seeing visions while studying Scripture. The men gained considerable influence on Müntzer and his congregation, and were christened as prophets. A year later, Müntzer and his small band of prophets traveled to

Wittenberg to convince the Lutheran reformers of the importance of relying more on the Holy Spirit. Some of the leaders took their words to heart, but Luther ran them out of town.

Later Müntzer reportedly remarked, "I wouldn't trust Luther even if he had swallowed a dozen Bibles."

"I wouldn't trust Müntzer," Luther retorted, "even if he swallowed the Holy Spirit, feathers and all."

Müntzer's teachings, however, struck a chord with many people in his day. His emphasis on the "inner word" of the Spirit, the significance of direct revelation from God through dreams and visions, the need for guidance from the Holy Spirit, and the necessity of the baptism of the Holy Spirit in order to discern spirits and interpret Scripture, helped him gain a significant following. Especially among the peasants.

Unfortunately, Müntzer craved not only spiritual power but political power. Within four years, Müntzer's fanaticism resulted in a revolt between his "Spirit-led" peasant followers and the city authorities. The peasants were massacred and Müntzer was beheaded.[3,4]

Although present-day Anabaptists (Mennonites, Amish, Church of the Brethren, among others) consider Müntzer a pockmark on their early history and avoid any association with him like the bubonic plague, they cannot deny his influence. The Anabaptists participated in a grassroots renewal movement that began with a heavy influence on relying on the Holy Spirit and laypeople exercising their spiritual gifts within the body, in addition to clergy and evangelism.

Lessons Learned From Our History

When I survey the history of the renewing work of the Holy Spirit in the church, several lessons come to mind:

The Holy Spirit never stopped working. Although I've only mentioned a few examples from church history, I could have included many more. By studying the renewing work of the Holy Spirit before the twentieth century, I'm struck by God's continual efforts to renew his church. Although they waxed and waned, "charismatic" gifts like prophecy, tongues, and healing never ceased. While the use of these gifts shouldn't be used as the definition of renewal, they often point to it.

The Holy Spirit has been at work since creation. He appears in Genesis 1 and continues working with the same intensity. He existed in the Old Testament and was actively at work *before* Pentecost just as he was during Pentecost. In the same way, he ministered with conviction and in power *during* the "spiritual dark ages"—before Agnes Ozman—just as he does today.

We stand on the shoulders of spiritual giants. While our faith is built on Jesus Christ, the practice of our faith and our understanding of it is built on the people who have gone before us. Spiritual movements, practices, and our understanding of God—every aspect of the Christian life—never arise out of a vacuum. Agnes Ozman's experience with the Holy Spirit resulted from the influences of the Holiness Movement in the late nineteenth century, which was rooted in the teachings of John Wesley from the eighteenth century, who was shaped by the Reformers of the sixteenth century, who were inspired by the Waldensians of the twelfth century, and so on, back to the New Testament church.

What does this mean to us? We have, at our disposal, the gleanings of over two thousand years of insight into God and his ways. We owe a great debt to men and women of faith who appeared before Agnes Ozman. God has bestowed upon us a wealth of wisdom from recent spiritual giants, such as Andrew Murray and R. A. Torrey, and even further back to Thomas à Kempis (fifteenth century), Hildegard of Bingen (twelfth century), and St. Augustine (fourth century), to name a few. It's okay to read books by people who are still alive (or you wouldn't be reading this book!), but let's not neglect legitimate spiritual giants whose writings have stood the test of time.

In the same way, as we study church history, we discover that many of the challenges and false teachings we face today have appeared sporadically since the first Pentecostal movement (in Acts 2). Why repeat their mistakes and struggles when we can avoid them?

The charismatic movement is one of many renewal movements. Many of us want to believe that the charismatic movement is different. But as we study the history of church renewal, we discover that renewal movements have much more in common than differences. Most begin with a deep conviction of one's sin, result in a commitment to repentance, thrive because many people exercise their spiritual gifts, and grow because vibrant believers enthusiastically share the Gospel. And they all find themselves replaced by newer renewal movements—the result of the Spirit's ever-creative work.

When looking at church history, we realize that the charismatic movement has yet to outlive a few of the renewal movements of the past. Who knows what it will look like in one hundred, two hundred, or even three hundred years?

What we do know is this: The charismatic movement is one of many moves of God that, in his grace and mercy, he uses to draw us closer to him. Rather than apologize for the excesses or boast in its successes, let's learn from the past, separate the good from the bad, and thank him for giving us glimpses into his love and power.

And while we're on the subject of power . . .

CHAPTER 5

We're Here to Pump . . . You Up!

Our Hunger for Hype and Thirst for Power

John Rambo of the *First Blood* movies was my hero in college. The first movie was okay, but the sequel rocked my world. I didn't care that the second installment won four Razzie awards ranging from worst picture to worst actor. Sylvester Stallone's character, John Rambo, embodied the Christian I wanted to be: lean, mean, and self-reliant.

How could anyone not like the movie taglines? "What most people call hell, he calls home." Or, "They sent him on a mission and set him up to fail. But they made one mistake. They forgot they were dealing with Rambo."

Lest you forget the plot, John Rambo, a disillusioned retired Vietnam veteran, frees a group of long-forgotten American POWs in Vietnam—and kills fifty-seven men in the process. Although I wince at the violence today, when the 1985 movie appeared in theaters, I considered it violent fun. What can I say? I was a college student!

To me, *First Blood* was an allegory of the Christian life, and I was the sanctified version of John Rambo. I even included my chosen nickname on the back of my intramural sports jersey: "God's Rambo"—fighting alone against the forces of spiritual darkness on the front lines of hell. Tearing down spiritual strongholds. Going where no other Christian has gone before.

Sent on a mission and set up to fail. But they made one mistake. They forgot they were dealing with *God's* Rambo.

Power-Hungry People

What was my prayer? *God, give me more power.* Every good charismatic knows the charismatic theme verse: "You will receive power when the Holy Spirit comes on you" (Acts 1:8). Keeping in step with our theme verse, we longed for power. Power to be witnesses. Power over the Enemy. Power over sickness and sin. Power to break generational curses. Power through prayer.

In the earlier days of the charismatic movement, we didn't care so much about political power because we knew it was no match for the power of God (perhaps we need to return to our roots!). In church we sang songs like "More Love, More Power" and "Show Your Power." We brought our unsaved friends to see the Power Team. We read John Wimber's books *Power Evangelism* and *Power Healing.*

I once attended a workshop conducted by a non-charismatic seminary professor who tried to explain the charismatic movement to a group of other non-charismatics (I attended in disguise). "The pursuit of the charismatic and Pentecostal is replication of the experience," he explained. *Is he crazy?* I thought. *The pursuit of the charismatic and Pentecostal is power.*

The thirst for spiritual power. Tongues might be the litmus test of a true-blue charismatic, but what we craved was power. The charismatic movement is more about power than anything. If you doubt it, just browse through the charismatic section of your nearest Christian bookstore.

All too often, Christians read the Holy Spirit's exploits in Scripture—miracles of healing and deliverance—and then set their Bibles down and live as if the God of the Bible no longer exists. Charismatic or non-charismatic, if we're honest, many of us would have to admit that we live as functioning agnostics.

The charismatic movement explained through Scripture and demonstrated through experience the tangible reality of God's power and his surpassing ability to overcome any sickness, disease, hopeless situation, or weapon in Satan's arsenal. God interacts with our everyday lives via the ministry of the Holy Spirit. Through my participation in the movement, I learned that God "is able to do immeasurably more than all we ask or imagine, according to his power that is at work within us" (Ephesians 3:20). Because of this, we always have hope.

Reflecting on this reality, however, leads me to some important questions. How do I get more of this power? What does this power look like? Why do I want it? And what's the purpose of the power?

Hans and Franz Were Charismatics?!

At times our attempts to tap into the Holy Spirit's power resembles Hans and Franz from *Saturday Night Live*: "We-ah he-ah to pahmp . . . [CLAP!] . . . you ahp!"

In college, a Christian speaker challenged us to "read the red and pray for the power." In other words, read Jesus' red-letter words in the Gospels and pray to minister in the same power as he did. So I compiled a list of favorite power verses, like Matthew 11:12, Matthew 12:29, and Luke 10:19, to pump me up. Whenever I felt discouraged or sick, I read or recited them over and over, believing they would infuse me with more power.

At church, when the senior pastor wanted to pump up the congregation, the band turned up the volume, we sang a little louder, jumped a little higher, and showed a little more enthusiasm, and then he yelled at us for an hour. Sometimes it even felt like somebody nudged up the thermometer a notch or two.

Then the power would fall. Either that or we just got a little sweaty.

But is that how God pours out his power?

Paul didn't seem as concerned with theatrics or calisthenics. He wrote, "My message and my preaching were not with wise and persuasive words, but with a demonstration of the Spirit's power" (1 Corinthians 2:4). Paul's description of his preaching tells us that he wasn't a dynamic speaker—nor did he want to be one. Nevertheless, the Holy Spirit showed up without requiring someone to prime the pump.

As a young youth pastor, I attended a national youth workers conference, with John Wimber as the final keynote speaker.

"I know many of you here feel empty, worn out," he said. "If you want to be filled up again, why don't you come forward and let's see what God has for you."

About a third of the audience walked to the front.

"Now we're going to wait on the Holy Spirit." People stood there for minutes, waiting in silence. *Why doesn't he do something?* I thought. But John Wimber never said a word. The band never played. Nobody clapped.

Then a person nearby started weeping. Then another. Then another person dropped to the ground, slain in the Spirit. By the time the meeting ended, most of the people at the front were either weeping or lying on their backs under the power of the Holy Spirit. Wimber, however, hardly said a word, and hadn't laid a hand on anybody.

God doesn't need someone to whip the crowd into a frenzy in order to pour out his Spirit.

We Already Have What We Seek

How do you tap into the power of the Spirit? The Holy Spirit isn't something you get. If you belong to Jesus, then the Holy Spirit already lives in you.

> His divine power has given us everything we need for life and godliness through our knowledge of him who called us by his own glory and goodness.
>
> 2 PETER 1:3

> For God gave us a spirit not of fear but of power and love and self-control.
>
> 2 TIMOTHY 1:7 (ESV)

Notice that both passages refer to the Spirit given to us as past tense. In other words, what we seek already lives within us. The Spirit is already at work in our lives, regardless of anything we do to manifest his presence.

In 1 Kings 19, Elijah didn't encounter God's presence in the wind, earthquake, or fire. He encountered him in a gentle whisper. Our problem isn't that we fail to do enough to usher in God's presence. All too often, our problem is that we fail to turn down the volume of our lives enough to hear his gentle whisper.

Lest we place him in a box, the Holy Spirit can work in dramatic ways, too. Elijah's encounter with God in a gentle whisper was preceded by a power encounter between him and the eight hundred and fifty prophets of Baal and Asherah. On Mount Carmel, before the people of Israel, fire from heaven struck Elijah's water-drenched altar, proving that Yahweh is God. A simple prayer answered by a powerful God. It should be pointed out that Scripture describes the pagan prophets as shouting, dancing, and frantically prophesying.

Power Comes Through Weakness (Really!)

Oftentimes we live as if God only pours out his Spirit on Scripture-quoting, overcoming, unrelenting "God's Rambos," who stand alone in battle and slay the dragons. We believe this because we want to follow a messiah who calls down fire from heaven on anyone who resists him (see how he responds to the request in Luke 9:51–55). We want demonstrations of unmistakable power because any show of weakness concedes defeat.

This, however, doesn't coincide with the primary way God pours out his Spirit. He doesn't need our blood, sweat, and tears. At Pentecost, the believers waited in the Upper Room forty days for the promised gift of the Holy Spirit. Although they prayed (Acts 1:14)—which was good—Jesus only commanded his disciples to wait (Luke 24:49; Acts 1:4). Somehow, he "forgot" to include the command to pray. No one sat in the back of the room playing an organ. No one led the group in rousing worship choruses. They waited. Prayerfully.

Paul wrote that he didn't preach the gospel with words of human wisdom "lest the cross of Christ be emptied of its power" (1 Corinthians 1:17). Our attempts at priming the pump actually hinder the power we seek.

Furthermore, he writes, "I want to know Christ and the power of his resurrection and the fellowship of sharing in his sufferings, becoming like him in his death" (Philippians 3:10).

Paul wanted to *know* Christ in the power of his resurrection, but he wanted to *become* like Christ in his death. Most of us want to know Christ and the power of his resurrection, but if we can be honest, few of us relish the idea of sharing in his sufferings, becoming like him in his death.

The two most significant days on the charismatic calendar are Easter and Pentecost. We love the resurrection and the outpouring of the Holy Spirit, but we don't know what to do with Good

Friday and the cross. Lent, to charismatics, is that stuff you empty out of the filter in your dryer. (For those of you deeply ensconced, Lent commemorates the forty weekdays between Ash Wednesday and Easter.)

In the ultimate act of weakness, Jesus offered himself on the cross for us. Now he invites us to join him.

> But [Jesus] said to me, "My grace is sufficient for you, for my power is made perfect in weakness." Therefore I will boast all the more gladly about my weaknesses, so that Christ's power may rest on me. That is why, for Christ's sake, I delight in weaknesses, in insults, in hardships, in persecutions, in difficulties. For when I am weak, then I am strong.
>
> 2 CORINTHIANS 12:9–10

Although he demonstrated signs and wonders unparalleled in human history, Jesus' ministry of power culminated in his crucifixion. It's no mistake that the symbol of the early church wasn't an empty tomb, but a cross.

In the same way, the symbol of spiritual power isn't a sword, but that old rugged cross. Not only Jesus' cross, but our cross—despite our craving for hype and drama.

What does true power look like? Weakness. Insult. Hardship. Persecution. Difficulty. Not everyone is blessed with the spiritual gifts of healing or prophecy, but anyone can suffer the above adversities. Although they seem to be antithetical to our pursuits, our weaknesses create room for Jesus to make his presence and love unmistakably clear.

This is good news for the masses that sought to "read the red and pray for the power," yet never experienced an out-of-body revelation of Jesus or a manifestation of his healing virtue.

To be sure, God manifests his power through extraordinary miracles of all kinds. But perhaps we've narrowed our definition of God's power so much that we overlook the purpose behind it.

The Purpose of the Power

As I evaluate my power pursuits, I'm forced to ask myself, *Why do I want it?* Two answers immediately come to mind:

- To take back what the devil stole
- To be used by God

Both are worthy pursuits, but I doubt they're the answers God is looking for. When I dig deeper, other answers surface:

- To prove to God that I'm worthy of his love
- To demonstrate to my friends and family that I'm significant
- To convince myself that I'm a "good enough" Christian
- To maintain control of my life and prevent anything bad from happening

Although embarrassing and incriminating, these answers probably better reflect the true me than the previous answers.

But what answer is Jesus looking for? Harking back to Philippians 3:10, he wants us to know him. He wants us, the conduits of his power, to know him—and he wants the people around us to know him.

I fear at times, in our pursuit of power, we lost sight of Jesus. We tried so hard to be used by him that we pursued Jesus' power more than his person. Jesus became a means to the power rather than the power becoming a means to knowing Jesus.

God's power inspired many of us to delve further into his ways.

However, craving his power only drove us away from our hearts' truest desire: Jesus.

Jesus embodied the perfect blend of spiritual power, authority, and character. But what do you do when a follower of Jesus embodies the first two ingredients but lacks an adequate supply of the third?

Read on . . .

CHAPTER 6

Touch Not God's Anointed

The Prevalence of Excessive Authority

Pay attention to the lyrics of their songs, and it won't be long before you notice their experience in—if not fascination with—Christianity. Move closer, and you may even detect on the breath of one of the world's greatest rock bands the aroma of new wine.

While in their early twenties, Bono, Larry Mullen, and The Edge—members of the rock band U2—joined an independent charismatic community in Ireland called Shalom Fellowship. Like many charismatic churches in the 1970s and early '80s, Shalom Fellowship was experiencing a powerful revival. The band's encounter with the Holy Spirit through this church left indelible marks on their lyrics, most evident in their albums *Boy* and *October*.

"I have spoken with the tongues of angels," Bono confesses in his song "I Still Haven't Found What I'm Looking For." But why hasn't he found what he's looking for?

If you've been around charismatics long enough, you will remember the long-ranging influence of the Shepherding movement. Through their magazine *New Wine*, Ern Baxter, Derek Prince, Charles Simpson, Don Basham, and Bob Mumford instructed churches filled with young believers how to disciple their flock. Through their proposed framework of accountability, they instructed every believer to submit to another person in greater spiritual authority.

At the top of the heap stood the pastor of the local church—the shepherd, in their terminology—who theoretically submitted himself to other shepherds. Any significant decisions made by anyone in the church, the Shepherding leaders taught, must be approved through this divine system of authority. At their height, more than a hundred thousand people participated in this movement, including Shalom Fellowship.

While U2 toured between 1981 and 1982, a person at their church claimed in a prophetic word that God wanted the band to break up so they could do something more "spiritually edifying." When the band returned home, their community was divided about whether the band should continue. The controversy devastated the band members, who relied on Shalom Fellowship as their spiritual lifeline.

Due to the pressure exerted by the leaders in spiritual authority over them as well as their friends in their Christian community who submitted to that authority, the three members of U2 walked away from Shalom Fellowship and their association with the organized church. Bono later commented, "I have this hunger in me . . . everywhere I look, I see the evidence of a Creator. But I don't see it as religion, which has cut my people in two. Religion to me is when God leaves—and people devise a set of rules to fill the space."[1]

Absolute Power Corrupts . . . Absolutely

Like death and taxes, reports of charismatic leaders abusing their authority are inevitable, if not daily occurrences. Like a charismatic Molotov cocktail, spiritual authority, charismatic gifts, and a captivating personality make for a potent mixture that can yield disastrous, volatile results.

But abuses of authority don't always involve concerns as noble as those of Shalom Fellowship. A recent story in the *Denver Post* exposed the dealings of a charismatic megachurch's senior pastor whose vast empire:

- Pays him an estimated annual salary of $750,000, enabling him to live in a $1.4 million home in a gated community while driving luxury vehicles and flying in the church-owned jet.

- Channeled real estate commissions to a daughter-in-law through their involvement in a government program that helps poor families renovate their homes.

- Created a public platform promoting a network marketing business his third wife and son operated that sold wellness products and recruited salespeople."

Similar abuses in spiritual authority among charismatics exist outside of churches. Television ministries regularly face accusations that they bilk their viewers of exorbitant sums of money and then spend it on extravagant items. Decades ago, financial controversies involving charismatic luminaries like Oral Roberts, Jim Bakker, and Jimmy Swaggart rattled the evangelical world, disillusioning their followers and altering the perception of Christianity among non-Christians worldwide. Following in their footsteps, Richard Roberts (Oral's son), Creflo Dollar (now there's a name for a television evangelist!), and Joyce Meyer have come under scrutiny in recent years.

When their financial dealings came under the microscope of the press, many of them shouted, "This is a spiritual attack!"

Nevertheless, many charismatics support the questionable actions of the people they follow. Once while discussing with a woman in my church the shady financial practices of a television evangelist, she responded, "How can that television program expose a man of God? Don't they know what Scripture says? 'Touch not mine anointed'" (Psalm 105:15 KJV).

When someone in authority over you speaks for God, how do you respond? When people with an aura of spiritual authority "hear" from God and promise a special blessing when you give, what do you do? You have no recourse.

Or do you?

The Flannelgraph Shepherd Will Never Lead You Astray!

In an informal poll I've conducted over the years, I've found that the vast majority of people I know who left the charismatic movement did so because someone in authority hurt them. Either someone pressured them to submit to a decision against their wishes, or the actions or decisions of a church leader (usually a pastor) hurt them.

First of all, let's be honest: God didn't design the body of Christ to be a free-for-all. Nihilists need not apply. He established an order to the church for good reason. The writer of Hebrews wrote, "Obey your leaders and submit to their authority. They keep watch over you as men who must give an account" (Hebrews 13:17). If I could have a nickel for every time someone quoted that passage to me, I'd be able to support my own television ministry.

Although it doesn't appear in the original Greek text, the NIV translation adds the word *authority* in the passage. Literally translated, the passage reads, "Obey your leaders and submit, for they watch over your souls as ones who must give an account." Adding the word *authority* gives significant power to the scope of a leader that the author probably never intended.

What intrigues me most in this passage is the meaning behind the word *watch*. The Greek word *agrypneo* means "to be awake," "watch over," or "care for," and it relays the idea of protection more than direction. A good pastor protects the congregation from disguised attacks involving division, deception, heresy, or fraud. In biblical times, this approach to leadership best described the role of a shepherd.

Psalm 23 elaborates on this idea. According to the psalm, a good shepherd:

- Leads the sheep to green pastures and quiet waters (verse 2).

- Guides the sheep in the paths of righteousness for his name's sake (verse 3). In other words, the shepherd walks ahead of the flock, pointing them to God.

- Protects and comforts the sheep (verse 4).

If you want to know what a good shepherd looks like, look at Jesus. He said, "I am the good shepherd. The good shepherd lays down his life for the sheep" (John 10:11). If you've ever watched a shepherd leading a flock of sheep (remember those old *National Geographic* specials?), the shepherd never exerts excessive authority or control. He never forces the sheep to follow behind in a single file line, nor does he beat the sheep when they stray off the path. And when a sheep wanders away, the good shepherd leaves the ninety-nine in search of the one (Matthew 18:12).

If you grew up in the church, you probably remember the flannelgraph figure of the shepherd sitting on a hilltop, watching the sheep while they graze in a grassy field. His goal? To protect them from attack. Protection more than direction.

What motivates the sheep to obey and submit to the good shepherd? Trust. The sheep know the shepherd has their best interests in mind.

But the shepherd analogy breaks down at some point. Jesus is the only *good* shepherd; the rest of the "undershepherds" (read: your pastors) have flaws—some more than others. Undershepherds are apprentices who make mistakes.

Like you and me.

For this reason, the apostle Paul likened the church to the body of Christ. All of us are members of the body of Christ, while some hold an office like pastor or teacher. Others—equally gifted, but not gainfully employed by a church—operate in gifts such as service, exhortation, mercy, or even pastoral care. But who is the head of the body?

> And [Jesus] is the head of the body, the church; he is the beginning and the firstborn from among the dead, so that in everything he might have the supremacy.
>
> COLOSSIANS 1:18

Our heavenly Father appointed Jesus—not the pastor—to be the head of the body. News flash! God never intended the life of the church to revolve around the pastor. Nor should it revolve around the body. The intended focus of the church is Jesus, its head. If pastors are equal members with the rest of the body, then they cannot assert themselves above the others, claiming to answer directly to God. Pastors must give an account to God regarding their pastoral responsibilities, but they nevertheless must be accountable to the rest of the body.

How to Evaluate Television Ministries

So where do television ministries fit into all of this? They don't. And that's part of the problem. Obviously, television didn't exist back in the day, so the closest comparison we can make to television preachers are the traveling apostles, teachers, and prophets in the early church. Apollos is probably one of the more recognizable New Testament names. A colleague of Paul, he preached in Ephesus and Corinth, and likely other cities.

Paul's affirmation of Apollos' ministry (Titus 3:13) tells us that traveling preachers weren't necessarily perceived negatively—

although Scripture warns against false teachers (2 Peter 2:1–3). In the same way, television ministries shouldn't be considered bad.

While not divinely inspired, a document called the Didache (pronounced *did-uh-kay*) served as an operations manual for churches in the early second century—which places it within a generation of the completion of the last New Testament book. The Didache offered instructions on a variety of subjects, including how to deal with traveling apostles and prophets. Here are a few nuggets of wisdom from this document that could also apply to television ministries:

- Every visiting apostle should be received as if God sent him.

- People who receive spiritual nourishment from the person's teachings should give him financial support.

- Any traveling apostle who asks for money is a false prophet.

- Don't listen to a prophet who does not live what he preaches.

- Beware of people who want to make a business proposition out of their Christianity.

Running them through this grid, some television ministries look good and some fail miserably. My suggestion: Give generously to the ministries that give you solid biblical food and pass the Didache test. More important, do not support any ministry that spends an inordinate amount of time asking for money or answering questions about indiscretion.

Recovering If You've Been Hurt by a Person in Spiritual Authority

If you've been involved in the Christian community for any length of time, someone in spiritual authority likely has hurt you.

Perhaps the person offended you, gave you bad advice, deeply disappointed you, or heaped condemnation on you . . . the possibilities are endless. Although it doesn't justify what was done, you're better off expecting it rather than being surprised by it. Obviously, examples of extreme abuse should never be expected nor tolerated without appropriate legal action. However, remember that Jesus handed the reins of the church to fallible people like you and me.

Christian leaders in the charismatic movement cannot avoid smelling like strange fire, because their ministries undoubtedly contain elements of both Spirit and flesh. Chances are highly unlikely that everything you experienced from the spiritual leader was bad. So be thankful for the good and give yourself permission to let go of anything harmful. By viewing Christian leaders through this lens, you create space for God to redeem the abuse for your good and his glory.

When someone in spiritual authority hurts us, the pain often cuts deeply, lingering for a long time. Why can this happen? Out of our brokenness, we blindly follow persuasive men and women who speak for God and offer us a touch with transcendence. Rather than go to God ourselves, we take shortcuts by going to people who seem most like him. Charismatic leaders with spiritual authority fit this description.

In their early days, the people of Israel begged God for a king. Despite his reluctance to answer their request, he finally relented and said in effect: "If you want a king, I'll give you a king." And what did they get? Saul—a gifted but very flawed man (1 Samuel 8–9).

Who did God have in mind to be their king? Himself. In the same way, he wants to be our primary source of spiritual sustenance. We need pastors and other men and women who will point us to Jesus and protect us from danger, but we must establish a personal relationship with him.

Last of all, the power of authority lies not in the leader but in the follower. If you follow a leader who faces constant accusations of fleecing or abusing the sheep while refusing to submit to a higher human authority, you bear the risk of being hurt. The choice of following that person belongs with you.

Despite their flaws, we need Christian leaders who will shepherd the flock and lead the sheep forward. Recently, seemingly dormant offices such as apostle and bishop have surfaced, offering strong leadership and direction. Are we enjoying the revival of a biblical office or are we experiencing biblically manipulative ways of controlling people?

CHAPTER 7

Apostles and Prophets and Bishops . . . Oh My!

Something Old or Something New?

The mass of people gathered along the Arkansas and Texas borders—upwards of fifty thousand—counting the seconds for the clock to strike high noon, when the throng would swarm into the Promised Land. Entrepreneurs, merchants, and homesteading farmers (with families in tow) nervously waited to stake a claim on their promised 160-acre parcels purchased from the Native Americans.

Then the bugle of the cavalry sounded. That's *cavalry*, not *Calvary*. Horses, covered wagons, and people on foot rushed in and fanned out along the rolling prairie. Pregnant trains raced into the deepest reaches of the virgin Oklahoma territory, transporting passengers carrying only one-way tickets.

Harper's Weekly described the day as "one of the most bizarre and chaotic episodes of town founding in world history." In only half a day, two cities of at least ten thousand people—Oklahoma City and Guthrie Station—were born. Between noon and sundown, *Harper's* reported that "streets had been laid out, town lots staked off, and steps taken toward the formation of a municipal government."

What kept people from hiding out ahead of time and beating their competitors to the two million acres of free land? Nothing. Some historians estimate that as many as nine-tenths of the claims were registered illegally by interlopers who snuck in before the appointed time.

The Oklahoma Land Rush of 1889 reminds me of the power grab that often occurs in charismatic churches and ministries: Instead of staking claims involving titles to property, aspiring men and women stake claims involving titles of authority such as apostle, prophet, or bishop in order to assert themselves over people and churches. And occasionally their actions resemble the interlopers who snuck in before their appointed time.

Apostles and Prophets Are No Longer an Appendix in the Body

Not long ago, only three of the fivefold ministry offices mentioned in Ephesians 4:11 were affirmed and active in the Western church—evangelists, pastors, and teachers. Apostles and prophets, however, operated more like an appendix in the body.

Pentecostalism reaffirmed the gift of prophecy beginning in the 1900s, and by the 1980s, independent charismatic churches began establishing the office of prophet. Mike Bickle, former pastor of Kansas City Fellowship, modeled an open and honest means—at times by trial and error—of integrating the prophet into the life of the church.

A few years later, apostles emerged, led by former seminary professor Dr. C. Peter Wagner, the presiding apostle of the International Coalition of Apostles. Wagner, who holds a PhD in sociology, identified apostolic networks of charismatic churches not only in North America and Europe, but around the world.

Since you're this far into the book, I probably don't need to prove the legitimacy of these last two offices. If you participate in the charismatic movement, you acknowledge by default that all the spiritual gifts exist. Nevertheless, church leaders are just as susceptible to the effects of "strange and holy fire" as the people in their congregations. Both flesh and Spirit permeate their ministries—as they do any ministry.

Titles Don't Define Us

Maybe it's just me, but when I read magazine advertisements referring to "Pastor Jack Hayford" or "Evangelist Luis Palau," the titles don't faze me. But when I see a reference to "Prophet John Miles" or "Apostle Miles Johnson" (these names are purely fictional—please don't contact me!), a mass in the pit of my stomach forms and my spiritual garbage detector starts flashing on and off.

Although Paul referred to himself as an apostle, he never referred to himself as Apostle Paul. At times he needed to validate his apostleship in order to establish credibility with his readers (particularly in Corinth), but Paul didn't seem overly concerned about giving himself a title. The same applied to Simon Peter. Similarly, other leaders in the New Testament never referred to themselves as Prophet Agabus or Apostle Junia.

Titles carry a degree of authority and command a level of respect. They enable pastors to walk into any intensive care unit in any hospital, and grant police officers the right to search any car on the side of the road (with a search warrant signed by the holder of another title—a judge). Titles, then, shouldn't be considered evil.

They do, however, separate people from the masses. Off-duty police officers who expect free coffee and discounted donuts at Dunkin' Donuts while vacationing with their families in Fort Lauderdale undermine the credibility of their position. In the church, emphasizing the title of apostle, prophet, evangelist, pastor, teacher, or bishop creates a dividing line between the men and women "doing the stuff" and everyone else who watches from the sidelines. Titles remind everyone who's important and who's not as important.

In reality, the *function* of a pastor (or any of the other fivefold offices) is more important than the title. Just because a person carries the title of a pastor doesn't mean the person pastors people well. On the other hand, I know many people who serve the body of Christ as pastors yet never received nor requested the title. Which is more important—the title or the function? The answer is obvious.

So if a person functions as an apostle or prophet in the body, why do we need to make such a big deal about the person's title? And why must we know the person's name is *Apostle* Miles Johnson or *Prophet* John Miles? If I didn't know better, I would think Miles and John were trying to convince people of their importance— which sure comes in handy when you're trying to sell books and CDs and getting people to attend your convocation.

J. Lee Grady, the editor of *Charisma Magazine*, once traveled to China to interview leaders in the house church movement. One woman told Grady that she oversees five thousand churches in a rural area.

"Are you a bishop or an apostle?" Grady asked, trying to understand the terms they use.

"We do not use titles," she replied. "We just call each other brother or sister."

Men and women with true spiritual authority don't need a title to be used by God. Exerting spiritual authority by parading one's title smells like a church power grab, akin to the Oklahoma Land Rush of 1889. God's purpose in giving the apostle to the body was never to exert authority over the greatest number of churches and build the biggest apostolic network.

The most important character quality in Christian leadership is humility. Jesus said if you want to be great in his kingdom, you must be a servant. Jesus gave these words to his twelve apostles-in-training:

> You know that the rulers of the Gentiles lord it over them, and
> their high officials exercise authority over them. Not so with
> you. Instead, whoever wants to become great among you must
> be your servant, and whoever wants to be first must be your
> slave—just as the Son of Man did not come to be served, but to
> serve, and to give his life as a ransom for many.
>
> MATTHEW 20:25–28

Emphasizing titles and then utilizing them to host convocations that line our pockets and make a name for ourselves reveal that we may not yet have the strength of character to handle the pitfalls of ministry. Entourages, lavish lifestyles, and profitable ministries certainly don't resemble our chief apostle, Jesus (Hebrews 3:1). More important than building an international ministry, God values humility, obedience, and a heart committed to pleasing only him.

Paul condemned "super apostles"—people boastfully asserting themselves as apostles—calling them false apostles. They were powerful speakers who exploited the church. He, on the other hand, confessed that he wasn't a trained speaker and that he served the churches while laboring as a tentmaker (see 2 Corinthians 11–12).

Please understand, I am neither condemning the gift nor the office of apostle, and I'm not saying all current apostles leading apostolic networks are exploiting the church. However, the emphasis and authority given to apostles in some circles concerns me.

People gifted as apostles or prophets (or any other designation, for that matter) shouldn't need to remind people of the office they hold. Long before the prophetic and apostolic offices reappeared, people exercised the gift of prophecy and apostleship—they just didn't know it. And perhaps they didn't care.

Besides, our actions and offices do not define us. I am not a pastor or a writer. You are not a doctor or a lawyer or a plumber. If you belong to Jesus, the cross defines you. Even if you don't consider yourself a follower of Jesus, you are a child of God created in the image of the One who made you, loves you, and desires a relationship with you.

Fellow colleagues privileged to serve in vocational ministry: Let's deemphasize our titles and focus our energies on serving others and fulfilling God's calling on our lives. If you attend a church but lack a title, don't let the lack of a visible status symbol get in the way of God's plans to use you.

Every believer plays a role in the body of Christ. Some roles are more visible than others. Nevertheless, every part of the body is equally important (1 Corinthians 12:12–27).

You Say Potato, I Say Po-tah-to

Most everybody likes to take their digs at denominations. Independent charismatics surely do. Even people in denominations do. Denominations organize churches around a common theological view of Scripture, promote fellowship between member churches and church leaders, develop economies of scale for doing ministry (i.e., hosting joint youth conferences, planting churches, or supporting missionaries), affirm pastors for ministry, and provide a system of accountability for the congregations and their pastors.

Sounds like an apostolic network.

Although independent charismatics bristle at the thought of participating in a Protestant denomination, their apostolic networks behave like one. But that's okay!

Independence can be a church's greatest strength and greatest weakness. You can make quick decisions and change your theology or worship style practically overnight. But you also expose yourself to catastrophic events without the stability of a denomination to back you up. What happens if your pastor commits adultery, claims God told him it's okay, and no leadership structure exists to remove him? Or what if he looks at grape Kool-Aid during Communion one Sunday and declares that "it's time to jump on the spaceship and fly home"? Or what if an active participant in the church bilks the retirement funds of countless members, resulting in an angry congregation teetering on collapse?

It happens.

Like a denomination, apostolic networks can provide stability to churches without controlling them. They also supply a system of accountability for church leaders, although many networks need to do a little more work figuring out to whom their apostles are accountable. In the end, the fivefold offices in the church, as well as every other leadership role, must submit to the local body—including the modern-day apostles. Authority unchecked will inevitably result in unnecessary damage to people in the congregation.

Apostolic networks may be a sovereign move of God, but then again they may be nothing more than a fad. Time will tell, and at this point, they're very early in their development.

We've looked at the apostle and the role of titles in Christian leadership, but what about the influence of people with strong prophetic giftings? To what extent do we give them license to speak into our lives?

CHAPTER 8

A Prophecy for Me!

A Biblical, Commonsense Look at Personal Prophecy

Let me be totally up front: Prophets freak me out.

Growing up, most of the prophecies I heard in church were fairly innocuous. Coincidentally, the vast majority of these usually began with "Thus saith the Lord." Why did God always speak in King James English? I guess if it was good enough for the Lord of Hosts and the apostle Paul, then we ought to follow their lead!

Anyway, most prophecies avoided taking any risks and followed the same basic format: "Thus saith the Lord, I am your God and you are my people. I love you with an everlasting love. Draw close to me and I will draw close to you."

Prophecies like that didn't intimidate too many people. But sometimes mysterious people appeared at church—whom no one knew—proclaiming that a catastrophe was at hand. When I was a teenager, a woman stood up in church in the middle of the sermon and prophesied that a flood would destroy the entire city of Denver.

I guess God forgot that Denver sits on a gentle slope. If a flood of biblical proportions occurred in Denver, the people in Denver wouldn't be destroyed, the people in Kansas would!

But then there were people in my church, godly people whom I respected, who moved in the gift of prophecy. They rarely prophesied future events, but they keenly discerned the spiritual landscape of our congregation and spoke words from God directly into it.

People who cultivate their prophetic gift through prayer, trial and error, intense study of God's Word, and the slow formation of godly character pay a high price to offer their gift to the body. For this reason, they hold my highest respect—as does Paul (read 1 Corinthians 14).

From my perspective, God wires strongly prophetic people differently than everyone else. These creative people live in a world rich in symbols and often display gifts in music, poetry, or the arts. Although we may look at the same passage of Scripture, they will distill a much deeper meaning that I would otherwise overlook.

But what intimidates many of us about these prophetic people is their eyes. They seem to look right through you, right into the deepest places in your heart, the places you don't want anyone to see. These are the people who freak me out. Before I spend time with them, I usually pray a simple prayer like this: "God, I'm so sorry for all my sins. I promise I'll never do them again. Please, please don't tell Sharon what I'm really like!"

I guess my prayer proves the adage that confession is good for the soul. We all need a good spring cleaning now and then, so perhaps scheduling regular appointments with our prophetic friends will help us walk the straight and narrow. Anyway, I try to make everything right with God ahead of time so the bad stuff inside me won't distract the person.

When we finally meet, I carefully measure every word I say. And usually when I say something I think is profound, they give me a look that says, *I know something you don't know, but I'm not going to tell you because you can't handle it.*

My two biggest fears concerning prophetic people are exposure and manipulation. I don't want them to trumpet my sins to everyone within shouting distance (especially if they name the wrong sin), and I don't want people controlling me under the guise of "Thus saith the Lord."

In the early days of the charismatic movement, impropriety seemed much more common. But people like Bill Hamon, Cindy Jacobs, and Mike Bickle have provided biblical guidelines to keep prophetic people in check—at least the sane ones.

Prophets: Portents of Great Importance

Back in the day, miners brought canaries into the mines to monitor the air quality. The canaries chirped and sang all day long, but when carbon monoxide levels—undetectable to humans—rose too high, the birds stopped chirping because they couldn't breathe or, due to the noxious fumes, they had died. The canaries served as portents of danger.

In a similar way, prophets operate within the body like that little bird in the cage (although we hope they don't die when something goes amiss). As a pastor, I've learned to monitor the prophets in my midst. "Surely the Sovereign Lord does nothing without revealing his plan to his servants the prophets," we read in Amos 3:7.

Prophecy and prophets played a pretty significant role in the early church. In fact, the New Testament uses variations of the word 104 times. Paul encouraged the church in Corinth to stop fixating on tongues and instead desire to prophesy.

Personal Prophecy and Scripture

While charismatics rarely dispute the legitimacy of corporate prophecy, they do question the validity of personal prophecy. Is it biblical? And if it isn't, is the practice a sin?

First of all, it seems to me that not every spiritual practice in a church needs to be supported by Scripture. If that were true, then we should meet in Jewish synagogues wearing robes and singing songs more reminiscent of music found in an Islamic mosque than the contemporary music sung in charismatic churches. Besides, Jesus served wine at the Last Supper, yet most charismatic churches serve grape juice when they celebrate Communion.

Although the Old Testament names an assortment of prophets like Elijah, Isaiah, and Jeremiah, the New Testament names only a few. One overlooked prophet, however, serves as a great example because the book of Acts mentions him twice in completely different contexts.

In Acts 11, Agabus prophesied that a great famine would spread throughout the Roman world—which later occurred during the reign of Claudius between AD 46 and 51. This first example qualifies as a classic prophecy that would go uncontested in any charismatic church.

Later in the book, Agabus reappears and offers a direct prophecy to Paul:

> After we had been there a number of days, a prophet named Agabus came down from Judea. Coming over to us, he took Paul's belt, tied his own hands and feet with it and said, "The Holy Spirit says, 'In this way the Jews of Jerusalem will bind the owner of this belt and will hand him over to the Gentiles.' "
>
> ACTS 21:10–11

If a man borrowed your belt, tied his hands and feet with it, and then prophesied that you would be bound and handed over to the Gentiles, who might possibly take your life, would you say it's a personal prophecy? Absolutely.

Personal prophecy existed in the Old Testament, as well. Probably the clearest example is when Saul, the future king of Israel, asked the prophet Samuel to discern the whereabouts of his stray donkey (1 Samuel 9). Scripture doesn't condemn him for this practice nor does it condone it.

Personal Prophecy vs. a Personal Relationship With Jesus

Personal prophecy, while sparsely mentioned in Scripture, proliferates in charismatic circles. A well-trained prophetic team at church will never lack for hungry men and women in need of strength, encouragement, and comfort from God.

Legitimate, and even some illegitimate, prophetic ministries that offer personal prophecies to their supporters usually garner a significant following.

Turn on the television for an evening of Christian programming and you will likely be exhorted to call in to receive your personal prophecy—and while you're on the line make sure you give a sizable contribution, of course.

That personal prophecy flourishes like it does shouldn't be a surprise. As the modern age slowly fades into oblivion, we no longer need tangible proof of God's existence. We believe that creation points to a God who loves us and that God speaks to us through his Word. But we also want to know that he cares about us. About *me*. Believing that someone can speak to me on God's behalf no longer poses a huge jump in faith.

Through personal prophecy, God has spoken profoundly into some deep places in my heart. If I could, I would meet with my prophetic friends every week to receive a fresh word from God.

Therein lies the problem.

Personal prophecy can easily become a quick fix to solving

my problems and a shortcut to enjoying the fruit of a relationship with Jesus. Why should I pray when I can go to a prophet who will tell me what to do? And why would I want to pay the price of cultivating an ever-deepening relationship with Jesus when I can take advantage of someone else's?

When the prophetic words of another person substitute for our relationship with Jesus, we are resorting to nothing more than idolatry. When we rely on the words of a prophet to make decisions, we are practicing fortune-telling. This applies to anyone who speaks to you for God—your pastor, a deeply spiritual person in your congregation, or a television preacher.

A steady diet of personal prophecy can easily become an addiction that feeds our flesh. Devoid of the give-and-take of a relationship with Jesus, we begin to assume that it's all about us. Serving Jesus and others is optional.

Personal prophecy works well when we need periodic spiritual adjustments to our heart, an occasional encouraging word, or the confirmation of a decision we are making. But it should never operate as our primary means of knowing Jesus, hearing from God, or making decisions.

People Who Live in Glass Houses Shouldn't Throw Stones at Prophets

Basing our lives on the words of a prophet poses incredible risk and exposes us to unnecessary pain. What if a woman giving you a prophetic word speaks from her opinions or misreads what God wants her to say?

While in college I attended a praise and worship conference. During the concluding worship service, one of the key leaders walked over to me and a woman sitting next to me.

Looking at me, he began, "Mike, I sense the Holy Spirit resting all over you. And I tell you, my son, that I am giving you the songs of the Lord. And people will be healed as a result of the songs that I give you."

Then he turned to the woman next to me and said, "My sister, I see a home full of children who have no parents and you will be their mother. Great will your house be, because I will bless you with many children whom you did not bear."

Obviously, I didn't write down his words, but that's the gist of it. So what was I to make of the prophecy? I left with the distinct impression that I may end up writing praise and worship choruses and the woman would adopt a number of children.

So what happened?

The woman became a famous writer of praise and worship choruses, some which you likely know. I, on the other hand, adopted a cute little girl named Marina. Kelley and I continue to discuss the possibility of adopting more kids in the future (once we recover from the ones we already have!). In essence, the two prophecies were correct, just reversed.

Again, this is the nature of the strange and holy fire: Every time we encounter the Spirit, inevitably we will encounter an element of flesh. Regardless of the person's prophetic abilities or spiritual insights, the possibility always exists that the person speaking the prophecy could be wrong.

Skeptics demand that prophets must be correct 100 percent of the time or they should be stoned. But legitimate Old Testament prophets didn't always get their prophecies right, and they weren't stoned. Nathan the prophet assured King David of God's approval to build the temple, before God stopped him (2 Samuel 7). In 1 Kings 22, the prophet Micaiah initially promised success for King Ahab in his battle against the Arameans. Eventually the armies of Israel and Judah were defeated and King Ahab was killed in battle.

New Testament prophets didn't always get it right, either. "For we know in part and we prophesy in part," we read in 1 Corinthians 13:9. In order to minimize the pitfalls, Paul explained that after hearing a prophecy, "the others should weigh carefully what is said" (1 Corinthians 14:29). The Greek word translated "weigh carefully" is *diakrinetosan* (say that fast three times!), which means literally "let them sift." What does a person sift? The wheat from the chaff. The true from the false. The Spirit from the flesh. The holy fire from the strange fire.

Should we stone, then, the prophet who doesn't bat a thousand? Not on your life.

No matter how much we respect the prophet, we still must take responsibility for our actions. Communication through prophetic words can fall apart at every step of the process:

- The prophet could misunderstand the prophecy from God
- The prophet could misinterpret the meaning of the prophecy
- The recipient could misunderstand the prophet's words
- The recipient could misinterpret the meaning of the prophecy

What happens if the prophecy falls apart at more than one point? What if the prophet mistakenly directs the mistaken prophecy to the wrong person? As you can see, the possibilities for a prophecy to break down are endless.

So why even open ourselves up to the pain and disappointment associated with prophetic words?

Because God values it. And when it works, God can use it to encourage us, redirect us, and remind us that he loves us. Deeply.

God speaks to us primarily and most authoritatively through his Word, especially as we intersperse our reading of it with prayer and meditation. However, our filters—our biases, limitations on God, and other personal issues—often taint our ability to listen objectively. Personal prophecy enables us to hear from God without those normal filters. Granted, they come through other people's filters—but that's why we must test everything.

Recovering From Prophetic Abuse

You don't need to spend much time in the charismatic movement before witnessing some pretty odd behavior, overwhelming control, or even spiritual abuse as a result of prophecy. Perhaps you've even been on the bitter end of it.

Speaking for God is a weighty responsibility every person with a prophetic calling should take seriously. Unfortunately, some people gravitate to prophecy because it gives them authority and control over others.

Perhaps a "prophet" embarrassed you in a public forum or manipulated you to perform unmentionable things in the name of God. Maybe a person spiritually abused you to such a deep degree that you feel its long-range effects today.

If this describes you, read closely: Please don't blame God for the unnecessary pain or embarrassment inflicted on you. Although he may allow you to experience pain, he will never inflict pain in order to punish you, shame you, or break your spirit.

Scripture describes the nature of prophecy: "But everyone who prophesies speaks to men for their strengthening, encouragement and comfort" (1 Corinthians 14:3). Does it strengthen you? Does it bring you encouragement or comfort? If so, then the prophecy is likely from God. You may feel deep conviction—which draws you closer to Jesus—but it will never bring condemnation—which drives you away from Jesus. God never honors prophecy that is abusive or manipulative.

Second, remember that God can redeem even the most heinous prophetic abuse (see Romans 5:3–4). Regardless of its extent, offer your pain as a sacrifice to God and ask him to use it to make you more like Jesus.

Third, remember that prophets have feet of clay just like

yours—which means they need grace and forgiveness just like you. Prophetic people can operate out of their own fears, insecurities, and wounds. It doesn't justify their actions, but it helps explain them. Often when I struggle to forgive someone, Jesus' prayer to his heavenly Father reverberates deep within me: "Father, forgive them, for they do not know what they are doing" (Luke 23:34). May Jesus' prayer become your prayer.

Last, simply because people have abused the authority inherent to prophecy doesn't mean you should avoid it altogether. By rejecting it, you preclude God from using an important means to speak into your life. Next time you may need to use more discretion in what you do with the prophetic word (like praying about it and testing it against Scripture), but in the long run, you will benefit greatly from it. That is, if it enhances your existing relationship with Christ.

Let's be grateful for the people God has brought into our lives who have prophetic gifts, but let's also remember that they're human—just like us.

Speaking of people who are human like us, let's move on to televangelists and other charismatic personalities. . . .

CHAPTER 9

If I Become a Christian, Do I Have to Look (and Act) Like Them?

The Cult of Personality

True confession . . .

Sometimes late at night, after my wife and kids go to bed, I drag a chair close to our entertainment center so no one can hear, and I turn on the TV. After channel-surfing for a while, I finally drift into forbidden territory. It's a place I habitually warn myself that I need to avoid.

As my heart begins to race, a world of fantasy and imagination comes to life. Although the visual images and promises provide momentary stimulation, deep down I know they will never bring me true satisfaction. With the remote in hand and my thumb strategically positioned, I attune my ear to every noise in the house, ready to switch stations if anyone catches me in the act.

Finally, when I've seen enough, I press the power button on the remote and tiptoe to bed. And every time as I slink under the covers, careful not to awaken my sleeping wife, I feel guilt and self-loathing for my indulgence.

My trespass? Porn? Heavens no! Christian television.

From pinkish bouffant (or is that buffoon?) hairdos to handle-bar sideburns straight out of the old *The Wild, Wild West* TV show, Christian television offers a bizarre facsimile of our faith. Where else can you gawk at people who look like they were transported to earth from a schlocky parallel universe?

A friend of my wife began exploring the claims of Jesus. Because of her limited exposure to Christians, her perceptions arose primarily from glancing at religious television programs while channel-surfing. "If I become a Christian," she asked my wife, "do I have to look like them?"

Good question. Do we have to look like them, much less act like them? Do we even want to?

Suckling Up to the Ministry Cow

Like any caricature, I'm overstating my case to make a point. God has used many television ministries to reach the masses for the cause of Christ. I've attended solid, Spirit-filled churches that ministered on television, I've appeared on their programs, and I even graduated from a college whose greater fame was its television ministry.

Many television ministries operate with honorable motives. Yet none of them can avoid what is common to all of us: Every time we encounter the Spirit, we inevitably bump into the flesh. At times what appears to be a holy fire is nothing more than strange fire. Unfortunately, television ministries that confuse the two leave a trail of burn victims in their wake.

At the same time, these brush fires aren't limited to ministries on television. To varying degrees, traveling ministries and the charismatic megachurches that worship at the altars of their senior pastors contribute to this cult of personality.

So what causes so many charismatic churches to look to these magnetic personalities for their spiritual sustenance?

Because the charismatic movement consists of very independent churches, no unified voice or overarching authority exists to speak on our behalf. As a result, the most compelling personalities serve as our defining voice. Over time, the charismatic preachers who rule the airwaves become the models many of us aspire to follow. On a lesser scale, some traveling ministries and megachurch pastors follow in lockstep with these men and women.

But should they speak for us (and for God), and should they model to us the naturally supernatural Christian life?

Yes and no. God has called gifted preachers and teachers to guide us into an ever-deepening relationship with the Father, Son, and Holy Spirit. But Jesus is our model, not the person speaking to us on television or the radio, or preaching from the pulpit. When we confuse our favorite charismatic personality with Jesus, we set ourselves up for tremendous hurt and disappointment.

If you think the men and women on most nationally syndicated Christian television programs are just like you and me, think again.

Thomas Freiling spent ten years working as the publisher of a charismatic publishing company. During his tenure, he worked directly with many of the charismatic media personalities we know and love.

"The amount of money that flows into some of these 'nonprofit' ministries is unbelievable," he comments. "Most of the people on Christian television live very opulent lifestyles. I once visited a famous televangelist who ordered room service in his hotel room to avoid the crowds. He ordered multiple items of the most expensive food on the menu, more than he could eat. After he ate his fill, he threw most of it away."

Freiling says, "People in these circles charge all their everyday expenses to the ministry. One televangelist's wife told me, 'If I wear an outfit on television just once, I can charge it to the ministry.' They charge all their travel to the ministry, including their vacations. Their ministries even own their multi-million dollar homes—some with as many as 18,000 square feet."[1]

While many of these people live at the expense of their "ministry," the ministry often pays them a very equitable wage. That way, when people look at their lifestyles and question their income, they can answer, "My ministry pays me a moderate salary." Which, technically speaking, is true.

But that doesn't stop them from double- and triple-dipping from their ministries. Many, if not most, of the well-known Christian personalities form for-profit businesses that work on behalf of their ministries.

Imagine, for a moment, that you're a televangelist. Feels good, doesn't it? A major publisher has just released your most recent book, *My Riches at Christ's Expense*, which you'd like to sell . . . I mean, make available, to your TV audience.

Instead of purchasing your book through your ministry, your for-profit business purchases fifty-thousand copies of your book from the publisher at a 70-percent volume discount (costing you only $6 a book). Then you turn around and sell the book at the full retail price ($19.99) to your nonprofit ministry—which is supported by the gifts of its loyal supporters. By selling the books through your for-profit business, you profit almost $700,000 on the deal. Best of all, the books you just sold to your ministry are either sold on your Web site at the full retail price or given to new "partners" who send you sizable contributions. My riches at Christ's expense!

The for-profit companies will also manufacture teaching CDs and DVDs of your television programs and sell them to the ministry—at retail prices, of course. Some television ministries also form shadow companies that charge exorbitant fees to place advertisements and purchase programming time on television. As you can see, television ministries can be very profitable operations.

"What disappointed me most," Freiling laments, "was that the vast majority of the people I knew were more concerned about the business of ministry than the ministry itself."

Homespun—and Spinning Out of Control

The glamour and glitz of Christian broadcasting doesn't drive me to these clandestine peep shows in the middle of the night. Nor does the air of confidence or showmanship of other Christian personalities. What drives me is the teaching. Sometimes they offer tasty morsels from the Word of God that feed the deep places in my heart. Other times, though, I hear sermons that take Scripture out of context and at times, completely misrepresent it.

The last time I indulged, a charismatic superstar proclaimed that Job was a fool. With amazing dexterity, he explained why the author wrote—but didn't really mean—Job was "blameless and upright," "feared God and shunned evil," and the "greatest man among all the people of the East" (Job 1:1, 3).

"Job is the biggest fool in the Bible because he lived in fear," the exquisitely dressed man explained. "He *appeared* blameless and upright. People *perceived* that he feared God and shunned evil. And because of it, he was considered the greatest man in the East. But Job lived in fear. And we know this is true because when tragedy struck, he said, 'What I feared has come upon me.' "

For fifteen minutes, the preacher mesmerized me with his theological gymnastics. "Our tragedies," he explained, "result from our fears and negative confessions." He defended Job's friends who pointed to his sin as the reason for his sorrow—despite God's assertions that Job's friends were misguided, at best (see Job 42:7).

Somehow, the preacher neglected the point of the book of Job. In the end, God answers Job's critics and Job's request for an explanation: "Where were you when I laid the earth's foundation? Tell me, if you understand" (Job 38:4). Over the last five chapters of the book, God asks Job and then his friends to explain all of his ways.

For the last two thousand years, the church has collectively agreed on the point of the book of Job: Tragedy happens to us, but the task of explaining it belongs to God. Granted, Job may have feared that tragedy would sometime strike, but good, God-fearing, faith-speaking people experience tragedy like the rest of us.

Needless to say, I turned off the television and stomped off to bed (quietly!) before the sermon ended.

Not every sermon on television misconstrues Scripture like this one, although many come close. Then again, I've heard some biblically sound sermons, too, but not as many as I would like.

Many of these Christian personalities lack any formal theological education. Although they usually operate with a healthy grasp of Scripture, they likely have little knowledge of how Scripture has been taught and interpreted over the last two thousand years.

The most popular Christian ministries thrive because they understand the felt needs of their audience. Weaving homespun wisdom, practical application of God's Word, and marketing savvy, they connect with their loyal followers on a deep level. To many, these dynamic speakers serve as a mediator between us and God. We want these powerful men and women of God to pray for our finances, our health, and our unsaved loved ones. And when they tell us our financial gifts serve as a step of faith in answer to our prayers, we believe them.

But in light of the extravagant lifestyles, sometimes questionable business practices, and at times unsound theology, do you really want to be like some of them?

I didn't think so.

It Isn't Reality Television, It's Surreality Television!

Christian television isn't reality, it's *surreality*. If you skipped Art Appreciation class in high school or college you may not remember what surrealism is. Surrealism was a twentieth-century artistic movement that expressed the workings of the subconscious through fantastic imagery and the bizarre combination of unlike subject matter.

Years ago, the popularity of the movie spoof *Attack of the Killer Tomatoes* hinged on the reality that tomatoes are harmless. When tomatoes get mad and take vengeance on the people who consume them, well, that's downright surreal.

In the same way, personalities who pontificate from gold-encrusted platforms and claim to be just like you, well, that's downright surreal. Preachers who proclaim the power of God's healing to everyone who believes while hiding their physical infirmities and disabilities, that's surreal, too.

The lifestyles of some of these people aren't at all like ours. Some make ten to twenty times what most of us earn in a year and can spend financial gifts with reckless abandon. And as much as we'd like to think that they care about our gifts to the ministry, they don't know who we are from Adam. With their high volume of mail, many don't have the time to personally respond to every donor. Oftentimes they respond to none.

But it's also helpful to remember that Christian personalities also resemble us in ways we easily overlook. They wrestle with materialism like we do. They struggle with insecurities and cover them up like most of us. In other words, charismatic superstars struggle with their own version of kryptonite just like you and I do. Some have been blessed by God with amazing spiritual gifts of speaking, faith, and sometimes healing, but they nevertheless sin. So if you've ever felt duped by a smooth-talking Christian personality, welcome to the club!

Sifting the Wheat From the Chaff

Christian television isn't inherently evil. Nor are independent ministries and pastors of charismatic megachurches. When evaluating a church or ministry, I usually begin with the assumption that it operates with God-honoring intentions. However, a few guidelines help us separate nonprofit ministries with noble intentions from the ones that may have strayed into profit-making ventures with less-than-noble intentions.

Insist on financial accountability. If a church or ministry refuses to make their financial records public, common sense dictates that they're probably hiding something. The ministry of a well-known televangelist purchased a $20 million airplane. Under U.S. federal tax guidelines, travel on the jet must be used solely for ministry-related purposes, or the cost of the trip should be reimbursed. Later, a television news program revealed that the jet was also used to transport the husband and wife on ski trips and hunting junkets—at the expense of their donors. When asked about his use of the jet, the man accused the news reporter of trying to bring down his ministry. But he never directly answered the allegations.

The U.S. government does not require nonprofit organizations to make their financial records public. Part of this reasoning is based on the separation of church and state. Nevertheless, any ministry operating in integrity shouldn't balk when asked about its finances. If we have nothing to hide, then our finances should be an open book.

Expect personal accountability. When the press exposes the immoral practices of a ministry, we must resist the assumption that the person is under a spiritual attack from Satan or a witch hunt from the godless media. Where there's smoke, there's usually fire. Just because people exercise strong gifts of healing or teaching doesn't mean they live above reproach. Nor does it mean they have the integrity and character worthy of receiving your gifts. Any ministry worthy of our gifts of time and money must be governed by a board of overseers that isn't populated by family members or old cronies.

Value spiritual accountability. Just because the seemingly profound insight into Scripture fell from the lips of your favorite speaker . . . it ain't necessarily so. In fact, if no one has ever said it before, it's probably heretical.

On his second missionary journey, Paul preached in a Jewish synagogue in Berea. Despite Paul's stellar credentials as a very educated Pharisee, Luke records that "the Bereans . . . received the message with great eagerness and examined the Scriptures every day to see if what Paul said was true" (Acts 17:11). Regardless of how deeply you respect the person on television or in church, we all carry the responsibility of filtering everything we hear through the grid of Scripture. Paul didn't appear bothered by the Bereans' practice, and, in fact, the group flourished under those conditions.

If Paul freely allowed the Bereans to hold him accountable to Scripture, then no one should claim to stand above the accountability of others. Heresy thrives when the speaker is accountable to no one. The danger of independent ministries and churches is that many of their primary leaders answer only to God.

Resist giving under pressure. If a talking head promises you healing or a financial breakthrough because you mailed in your faith gift, assume the worst. High-pressure tactics are intended to convince you to give before you have second thoughts. And unusual but biblical-sounding ploys like the "Day of Atonement Offering" are merely creative approaches to separating you from your money. Remember the old adage: A fool and his money are soon parted.

Beware of perpetuating a personality cult. Magnetic personalities in the charismatic subculture tend to attract people who quote them more than Scripture. When we place men and women on such a high pedestal, we set them—and us—up for a fall.

Television and radio ministries should never serve as our primary source of spiritual nourishment. Nor should traveling speakers and preachers. Our personal relationship with Jesus, supplemented by generous helpings of fellowship, corporate worship, devotional Bible reading, and biblical preaching in the context of a local church are the meat and potatoes of our spiritual walk. The best some ministries can offer are the equivalent of a granola bar, or at worst, a junk-food binge.

If you feel betrayed or duped by a television ministry, vote with your remote. If a ministry doesn't line up with the aforementioned criteria, stop listening and stop giving. At best, you can laugh at your gullibility and determine to avoid indulging again.

However, don't become embittered by the men and women who took advantage of you. Remember that you and they share many of the same struggles.

CHAPTER 10

Why Don't We Just Outlaw Sin Altogether?

Navigating Our Way Between Legalism and Grace

Walk through a building in a well-known charismatic learning institution and you'll enter a corridor called the "Hall of the Apostles." One by one, paintings of Jesus' original twelve followers line the walls. Initially, the paintings look fairly normal, although the extremely youthful appearance of the men may seem a little odd.

Halfway through the display, you realize the reason for the men's apparent youthfulness: They're all clean-shaven—including Jesus! Proceed to the end, however, and one apostle sticks out like a journalist at a Benny Hinn crusade. His long hair and bushy beard compensate for all the other men in the lineup. You can probably guess the name of the hirsute intruder. It's Judas Iscariot, of course.

At this point, you may have surmised that the school enforces a strict policy with their male students, stipulating that the length of their hair cannot extend past the collar. And under no circumstances can they grow facial hair (neither rule applies to the female students!). No long sideburns. No goatees. Not even a mullet—despite the school's location in the South. Mustaches are permitted as long as the men keep them neatly trimmed and they extend no further than the length of the mouth. Samson, John the Baptist, and other Nazirites would be escorted off the grounds at this school on the first day of registration!

Ironically, the Hall of the Apostles links the library with the classrooms. A quick study in one of the many theological books in the library would reveal that beards and hair that strays beyond the collar were common in Jesus' day. In fact, going beardless was considered a disgrace.

Not surprisingly, after graduation many of the men grow their hair past their shoulders and allow their beards to flourish.

Let's Just Nip It in the Bud and Outlaw Sin!

Every culture establishes a code of conduct, behaviors, and practices—all couched within their belief system. Charismatics included. Some rights and wrongs stand firmly on the foundation of Scripture; others stand gingerly on the ever-changing sands of culture. The goal? To eradicate sin—at least to the best of their ability.

In the early 1900s, a faith healer named John Alexander Dowie founded a Christian community north of Chicago named Zion City, which eventually grew to six thousand people. In the city charter he outlawed sin.

Despite his best intentions, Dowie's efforts at eradicating sin fell short. The city exists to this day, but it never lived up to his expectations. Not even close.

But apart from outlawing sin, we often go to great lengths to minimize its influence, even if it means mortgaging a faith that rests on grace. In the end, we enforce laws that act as barriers between us and God. And in the hands of misguided leaders, they also serve as tools of control.

But let's suspend present-day reality for a moment and play one of my favorite games: Culture vs. Scripture. I'll list a series of present-day beliefs and practices, and you place a check mark under the appropriate column if it's supported by charismatic culture, Scripture, or both.

Beliefs and Practices	Charismatic Culture	Scripture	Both!
1. You should dress up when you go to church.			
2. During corporate prayer and worship, men should wear veils on their heads and women should avoid wearing hats.			
3. When you pray, always close your eyes.			
4. Faithful followers of Jesus listen to Christian music and abstain from listening to secular music, otherwise known as "devil music."			
5. Dancing in church is okay (as long as it's done tastefully), and dancing to "devil music" is . . . of the devil.			
6. Good Christians read their Bible and pray every day.			
7. Voicing our temptations and fears gives the devil a foothold into our lives.			
8. Tithing is strongly supported in both the Old and New Testaments.			
9. God promises to bless you whenever you give.			
10. God blesses the righteous more than the unrighteous.			
11. Good Christians are patriotic.			

To what extent are the beliefs and practices we hold closely based in Scripture and to what extent are they based in culture? If you run the aforementioned items through the grid of

Scripture, you may be surprised at the results. Here's my take on the answers:

1. You should dress up when you go to church.

Nothing in Scripture dictates that we should wear our Sunday best when going to church. Way-y-y back in the day, men and women wore the same robes to Saturday synagogue or Sunday church as they wore the rest of the week. The tradition of dressing up for church probably arose out of the desire to show God respect when people gathered for worship. But our outsides aren't necessarily accurate indicators of what's on the inside, as Jesus pointed out to the Pharisees in Matthew 23. *You can check this one off as "Charismatic Culture!"*

2. During corporate prayer and worship, men should wear veils on their heads and women should avoid wearing hats.

Trick question! Men don't usually wear veils. But seriously, in 1 Corinthians 11, Paul instructs the men to keep their heads uncovered and the women to keep their heads covered when they gather for corporate worship. *Technically speaking, you can't check any of the boxes because it's a trick question ("None" isn't one of the options). But Scripture does support women covering their heads and men keeping their heads uncovered.*

3. When you pray, always close your eyes.

Scripture doesn't tell us to close our eyes when we pray. Quick story: At my first summer youth group retreat, when I was thirteen, we arrived at the camp just in time to pray over our Monday lunch and then eat. After the prayer, my best friend leaned over and pointed to a man across the room. "Mike," he said. "I don't think that guy's a Christian because his eyes were open when we prayed." "That guy" was our retreat speaker! *Mark that "Charismatic Culture."*

4. Faithful followers of Jesus listen to Christian music and abstain from listening to secular music, otherwise known as "devil music."

Sorry to disappoint those entrenched in the Christian music scene. While positive, encouraging, and safe for the whole family, Christian music isn't our only scriptural music option. In fact, the Christian music industry didn't exist in Bible times. But on a deeper level, Scripture doesn't mention a difference between spiritual and secular. *Mark this one "Charismatic Culture."*

5. Dancing in church is okay (as long as it's done tastefully), and dancing to "devil music" is . . . of the devil.

Interestingly enough, dancing in church doesn't appear in the New Testament. In fact, limiting ourselves to "dancing to the Lord" isn't even supported by Scripture, considering David's embarrassing jig in 2 Samuel 6 and 1 Chronicles 15. Michal's criticism of David's exuberant display resulted in a lifetime of barrenness. But apart from that, Scripture seems to affirm dancing in contexts that aren't necessarily spiritual (Judges 21:21; Luke 15:25). *This one falls under the category of "Charismatic Culture."*

6. Good Christians read their Bible and pray every day.

While we're encouraged to study God's Word, nowhere are we commanded to read it every day. I'm not trying to get you off the hook, because reading your Bible is extremely beneficial, I'm just saying . . .

Prayer, on the other hand, isn't a daily command, it's a moment-by-moment command. Scripture repeatedly exhorts us to pray without ceasing (Luke 18:1; 1 Thessalonians 5:17; et al). *Let's mark daily Bible reading as "Charismatic Culture" and daily prayer as "Both."*

7. Voicing our temptations and fears gives the devil a foothold into our lives.

Confessing our sins one to another brings healing (James 5:16). The authenticity that comes from walking in the light creates true biblical fellowship (1 John 1:7). Walking in the darkness—hiding our temptations, fears, and sins—actually fosters an environment for the devil to continue his intention to destroy our lives (John 10:10). *This one's definitely "Charismatic Culture."*

8. Tithing is strongly supported in both the Old and New Testaments.

Tithing is strongly supported by the Old Testament, but appears in only three New Testament passages. Of those three appearances, two of the references—by Jesus—cast tithing in a somewhat negative light. If you don't believe me, look it up in Matthew 23:23 and Luke 18:12 (the third passage is Hebrews 7:5–9). The fact is, God doesn't own 10 percent; he owns 100 percent. *Let's file this under "Charismatic Culture."*

9. God promises to bless you whenever you give.

This is definitely true. All too often, though, we like to tell God what form of blessing he should give us in return and when he should give it (usually we want it *now*). Sometimes our definition of blessing looks much different than God's. Most of us like monetary rewards, which he sometimes gives us, but always, always, our gifts lay up treasures for us in heaven (Matthew 6:19–21). *This one belongs in the "Both" category.*

10. God blesses the righteous more than the unrighteous.

Again, it depends on how you define blessing. If you operate from the "accumulation of money and stuff" definition, then the most righteous people in the world would be the wealthiest, and the most evil people would be the poorest. But we all know that isn't true. Sometimes God blesses the righteous with good things like money or security. However, if we add an eternal dimension to our definition (i.e., eternal life, lives of significance, the opportunity to hear from God), then this statement is definitely true. *Let's place this one under "Both," with a notation that it depends on your definition.*

11. Good Christians are patriotic.

The early Christians weren't known to be patriotic. In fact, Roman emperors killed them because their allegiance was pledged to Jesus. This begs the question: Can we pledge our allegiance to more than one person or entity? It doesn't seem possible. So if we pledge allegiance to the flag, where does our allegiance to Jesus fit in? Just asking . . .

We are, however, commanded to submit, honor, and respect our governing authorities (Romans 13:1–7) and pray for them, as well (1 Timothy 2:1–2). *Please don't stone me or tell me I don't love my country, but this one belongs under "Charismatic Culture."*

If you want to interact with my answers, please visit my Web site: *www.strangefireholyfire.com.*

My purpose in offering this quiz is to show that determining what constitutes "holy living" isn't so easy to determine. Some of our values are based in Scripture, but more times than we'd like to admit, our values are built on the culture around us.

When I was a youth pastor, unchurched boys would come to my youth group wearing knit hats on their heads. Some of the older people at church saw the boys praying with their heads covered.

"Don't you know that it's disrespectful for those young men to wear hats when they pray?" one of the older ladies asked me.

In a rare moment of discretion, I bit my lip, because I wanted to say, "Let's make a deal: I'll ask the boys to take off their hats in church when you agree to wear a veil."

But on a deeper level, the "performance mentality" of living by a strict prescription of rules likely damages more people than it helps. When I was a teenager, I attended a youth retreat led by a speaker who literally tried to scare the "hell" out of the kids.[1]

"If you're having sex with your boyfriend or girlfriend in the backseat of your car," he warned us, "when Jesus comes back, he'll leave you here!"

By the end of the man's talk, certain teenagers in the room were distraught. It didn't take long to figure out who in the room was messing around.

What's My Line?

Now, I'm not advocating premarital sex, but something doesn't seem right when our salvation depends on what we do or don't do. At what point do we cross the line and lose our salvation? And what if we misjudge the location of the line? Even worse, what if we misjudge what constitutes the line altogether?

The camp speaker defined the line as premarital sex. Other leaders in my past defined it as drinking or not submitting to authority, and I have friends who were taught that the line was not speaking in tongues.

Jesus, however, moved the line to a place that should make all of us uncomfortable:

> You have heard that it was said . . . "Do not murder, and any-
> one who murders will be subject to judgment." But I tell you
> that anyone who is angry with his brother will be subject to

---

[1] Sorry for the digression, but have you ever noticed that you can write whatever you want if you just place quotation marks around it? It also works when you speak with someone if you make air quotes when you say the forbidden word. It's like doing something bad without having to take responsibility for it. It's also a great way to sneak forbidden words into Christian books!

judgment. Again, anyone who says to his brother, "Raca," is answerable to the Sanhedrin. But anyone who says, "You fool!" will be in danger of the fire of hell.

MATTHEW 5:21–22

Have you ever been angry at someone? Hello-o, are you human? Being angry doesn't necessarily mean throwing small objects or yelling at someone. It simply means you're mad. Maybe even justifiably mad. If so, you've already murdered that person in your heart.

If you stand on (or "hide behind") Ephesians 4:26, which says, "In your anger do not sin," you can take comfort in knowing that both the Ephesians passage and Jesus' quote use the same Greek word for anger—*orgizo*. For those of us who think we have our act together, it's a pretty sobering statement. But to make sure his listeners understood his point, Jesus stated it a different way:

You have heard that it was said, "Do not commit adultery." But I tell you that anyone who looks at a woman lustfully has already committed adultery with her in his heart.

MATTHEW 5:27–28

In both statements, Jesus levels the playing field for all of us. While I may not have committed adultery, I can't claim to have never lusted. Guilty as charged.

Jesus' words stick a dagger into the heart of our performance mentality.

God began weaning me from my performance mentality when I began realizing the full weight of Romans 5:8: "But God demonstrates his own love for us in this: While we were still sinners, Christ died for us." God didn't wait for us to get our act together before sending Jesus; he sent Jesus because we *didn't* have our act together.

Furthermore, Paul wrote in Ephesians 2:8–9 that "it is by grace you have been saved, through faith—and this not from yourselves, it is the gift of God—not by works, so that no one can boast."

All too often, I assume that my actions bring me into a right relationship with God. That I'm a better Christian if I fall in line and follow the rules. But that line of thinking directly contradicts the heart of the gospel.

A Word About the Law

Hundreds of books have been written about the relationship between grace and the Law. And frankly, I doubt I can even make something up that will contribute to the discussion. However, a few thoughts bear explaining about the nature of the Law.

The Law isn't bad. In Scripture, "the Law" refers to the first five books of the Old Testament. Jews, as well as Messianic Jews, refer to it by the Hebrew term *Torah*. The essence of the Law is distilled in the Ten Commandments (Exodus 20:1–17; Deuteronomy 5:6–21). Read through the Psalms, and you'll quickly discover that the psalmist loved the Law. The longest chapter in the Bible, Psalm 119, is a poem extolling the beauty of the Law.

Without a codified system of laws, society would run amok. Obviously, laws must be enacted for our protection. We need stoplights and stop signs so people won't run into each other at intersections. We need penalties for stealing or most retail establishments would go out of business. Without laws, anarchy would reign.

In the same way, Christians need a framework of behavior. After we give our lives to Christ, he doesn't give us a free pass, granting us the freedom to live as our flesh dictates. The apostle John wrote, "Everyone who sins breaks the law; in fact, sin is lawlessness" (1 John 3:4). Living apart from the Law is sin. We all need a code of conduct.

Jesus is the Law. Jesus maintained a peculiar relationship with the Law. As much as many of us enjoy living apart from the requirements of the Law, Jesus proclaimed, "Do not think that I have come to abolish the Law or the Prophets; I have not come to abolish them but to fulfill them" (Matthew 5:17). Furthermore, he said that "unless your righteousness surpasses that of the Pharisees and the teachers of the law, you will certainly not enter the kingdom of heaven" (Matthew 5:20).

If you grew up in a legalistic church, you probably know this last passage by heart—and it was used to control you. But can anyone surpass the righteousness of the Pharisees? Does anyone want to even try? Not on your life!

John, however, sheds light on how any of us can even think about getting into heaven. "In the beginning was the Word, and the Word was with God, and the Word was God" (John 1:1). Jesus was the Word. The *Logos*. The Law. Not only that, but "the Word became flesh and made his dwelling among us" (John 1:14). Jesus was, is, the embodiment of the Law. The fulfillment of the Law.

Hang in with me here; I have one more Scripture passage to throw into the mix. If you're a recovering charismatic like me, you know that Jesus died on the cross to forgive our sins. He died on our behalf. So where does he live now?

> To them God has chosen to make known among the Gentiles the glorious riches of this mystery, which is *Christ in you, the hope of glory.*
>
> COLOSSIANS 1:27 (ITALICS ADDED)

Christ lives in you! Jesus, the Word made flesh, the standard of the Law, the fulfillment of the Law, lives in you.

What does this mean for us? The deepest part in you isn't even you. It's Jesus. The truest you is Jesus. Despite any struggles you might have with compulsive habits, addictions, or shameful behaviors, the deepest part of you is not what you do. It's Jesus.

So what does this have to do with the legalism you might have experienced in the charismatic movement?

The deepest part of you wants to do good. That's not to say that the deepest part of you wants to follow the code of conduct of the day. It means that the deepest part of you wants to please God and enjoy an unhindered relationship with his Son, Jesus. Reminiscent of the psalmist's words in Psalm 42:7, "Deep calls to deep," the deepest part in us—Jesus—calls to the depths of our heart. And because he already lives there, he helps us find him and then please him.

You don't need the Law. Obviously, we all need traffic laws to keep things in order. But something inside us tells us the difference between right and wrong. It's Jesus, speaking to you through the conviction of the Holy Spirit. People who break laws, or at a minimum, care only for themselves, need the Law. You, however, don't need it, if Jesus lives in you.

The Law is Jesus living in you. An inward change has already been made in your heart. The process of that inward change becoming embodied in your life is called sanctification. Changes of this sort concern themselves with elements of our *character*: love, joy, peace, patience, kindness, goodness, faithfulness, gentleness, and self-control. It's the character of Jesus, the fruit of the Spirit's work in your life. But notice this: When Paul lists the aforementioned fruit of the Spirit in Galatians 5, he concludes by explaining, "Against such things there is no law" (Galatians 5:22-23).

No law is needed because you have the character of Jesus radiating through you!

In my experience, few Christians are able to distinguish the difference between the Law and legalism. Jesus is the Law, and he lives in you . . . if you have received him into your life.

Legalism, however, concerns itself with specific *behaviors*: hair length, dressing up in church, speaking the properly worded confession at the right time. Legalistic behavior rarely concerns itself with our character or our relationship with Jesus. It concerns itself more with a code of conduct than the state of our heart.

Clearly God wants us to avoid certain behaviors. But the standard we measure our behaviors against is the fruit of the Spirit. If the behavior doesn't violate the spirit of the fruit, it's probably okay.

Two final points I want to make about this: First, God evaluates our actions according to the intent of our heart. At first blush, that seems like a relief, because no one knows our heart—but it may cause us to blush when we realize that God does. He's more concerned about the "why" of our actions than the "what."

Second, living holy lives is a *reaction* as opposed to an *action*. Better yet, it's a *response*. "In view of God's mercy," Paul wrote, ". . . offer your bodies as living sacrifices . . . this is your spiritual act of worship" (Romans 12:1). Our lives are a grateful response for what Christ has done for us. This is called worship. If your actions were motivated by the desire to fit in and make God love you more, then they weren't worth a timeshare at Heritage USA.

Making Sense of Your Legalistic Past

If in your past (or even in your present), you were forced to carry a heavy yoke of legalism, please understand: God's love for you carries no conditions on what you've done—or not done—for him. To put it into the unforgettable words of Philip Yancey, "Grace means there is nothing we can do to make God love us more. . . . And grace means there is nothing we can do to make God love us less."

If it's helpful, take a few minutes to reflect and journal your answers to the following questions:

- Read Matthew 11:28–30. What difficult yokes or heavy burdens have been placed on your shoulders?
- What did they do to you? In you?
- Why did you agree to carry them?

- How do they line up with Jesus' words in this passage?
- What is Jesus asking you to do with them?

Now take a moment to pray, asking Jesus to remove the yokes and burdens you have been carrying. Then invite Jesus to fill the empty places in your heart that caused you to accept the yoke that was placed on you. Last of all, pray that God would engulf the people who placed these yokes on you with a renewed sense of his grace and mercy.

CHAPTER 11

We Don't Need No Education

Our Contempt for "Book" Knowledge and Pursuit of "Revelation" Knowledge

Part of my reluctance to remain in the charismatic movement involves the prospect of "living down" my education. An undergraduate degree from Oral Roberts University made for a credible charismatic résumé, but a graduate degree from a seminary somehow negated it. In fact, when I decided to attend a seminary, I chose one with some semblance of credibility among charismatics. Obviously, it wasn't credible enough.

While attending Fuller Seminary in Pasadena, California, I served as a youth pastor and worship leader at a small Pentecostal church. The flexibility of my work schedule and the friendliness of the congregation made it the ideal seminary job.

Periodically, a woman in the congregation would stop me just before the beginning of the worship service and ask, "How do you like that Fuller Theological *Cemetery?*" Needless to say, her inquiry went a long way in preparing my heart to lead the congregation into the Holy of Holies later that morning!

The dear woman was baiting me to see how I would respond.

If I reacted in anger, I would prove her point that seminary does nothing to change the character of a person. In that respect, she was correct, because it doesn't. But her occasional digs were also intended to relay the message that a seminary education would deaden my relationship with Jesus, which it didn't.

So I either ignored her derogatory comments or I asked her if she'd ever taken a seminary class (she hadn't), and then chirp in with a smile on my face, "Well, then, don't knock it till you've tried it!"

Russ Spittler, one of my seminary professors at Fuller, once lamented to *Christianity Today* about his experience with his Pentecostal denomination:

> In the Assemblies of God, when you apply annually for credentials, you have to identify your ministry: pastor, chaplain, missionary, evangelist, other. For years, I had to check "other." I was always an "other" because a teacher is not highly respected [so it's not on the list]. If the Holy Spirit is teaching you, why would you have any regard for this or that teacher?

Few people outside Christian publishing realize that a number of the Christian personalities we know and love don't write the books they purportedly author. They either lack the time or the skill (or both) to write a full-length book. And believe me, next to being married, writing a book is one of the hardest tasks a person will ever accomplish.

For a few years, I supported my family by writing books for several televangelists. Publishers hired me to ghostwrite books for various personalities in the charismatic movement. Their reason for enlisting me? I knew the charismatic market (my ORU education paying off), and with my seminary background, I could prevent their well-known charismatic authors from venturing into heretical waters (read: It saved publishers from having to pull books off bookstore shelves due to negative publicity, saving them bucket loads of money).

Consider the irony: Television preachers proclaimed they didn't need to be taught by anyone but the Holy Spirit, yet their publishers insisted that the manuscripts be rewritten by a seminary graduate.

Some of the televangelists handled Scripture in a very responsible manner. But occasionally—actually more often than I'd like to admit—they really messed things up. Usually, the biggest problems occurred when they delved into word studies. Exploring a Hebrew or Greek word in depth when you haven't formally studied Hebrew or Greek can get you into a lot of trouble. Imagine a professor in a medical school teaching their student doctors how to perform brain surgery when they had never stepped into an operating room. How confident would you feel if you were that particular doctor's patient? You get the idea.

Knowledge Puffs Up, but Love Builds Up

Charismatics and their Pentecostal cousins have historically shown contempt for formal education, claiming that "knowledge puffs up, but love builds up" (1 Corinthians 8:1). But if you closely examine the context of 1 Corinthians, you discover that Paul wasn't concerned that the Corinthians were spending too much time brushing up on their Greek exegesis. He was more concerned about their reliance upon what modern-day charismatics affectionately call "revelation knowledge."

In Paul's day, the church contended with a sinister heresy called Gnosticism. Gnostics believed in a dualistic world that differentiated between spirit, which is good, and matter, which is evil. Gnostics stressed the life of the spirit and avoided involvement with the material world. Many "Christian" Gnostics believed that Jesus ministered on earth without a physical body, because the body is evil. Instead, he was a spirit who appeared to have a physical body.

Gnostics gravitated into two camps. The first camp, believing that all matter was evil, tried to beat their bodies into submission through extreme ascetic practices. Paul addresses elements of this belief when he asks in Colossians 2:20–21, "Since you died with Christ to the basic principles of this world, why, as though you still belonged to it, do you submit to its rules: 'Do not handle! Do not taste! Do not touch!'?"

The other camp, believing that the body was beyond redemption, chose the opposite route. They followed the appetites of their flesh, indulging in illicit sinful practices, all the while believing that their physical actions did nothing to affect their spirits. The church in Corinth battled this particular heresy, which is evident throughout the book. For example, in 1 Corinthians 5, Paul scolded the Corinthians for tolerating a man who was living with his father's wife.

Salvation, to the Gnostic, concerned itself with attaining a special divine *gnosis*—the Greek word for knowledge—that others didn't, or couldn't, receive. People who received what they believed to be a special revelation from God strutted their spiritual superiority around the church in Corinth. It was into this context that Paul exhorted his readers, "Knowledge [*gnosis*] puffs up, but love builds up." So you see, Paul wasn't demeaning the importance of a solid biblical education, he was pointing out that revelation knowledge can cause people to become filled with spiritual pride.

Where did I learn this pertinent information? At seminary, of course. But without the proper understanding of the context, most people derive an opposite understanding of this Scripture passage.

In Praise of Knowledge

Despite the contempt among many charismatics for "head" knowledge, many at the same time relish the fact that the apostle Paul was one of the most theologically educated men of his day.

During his missionary travels, Paul continued identifying himself as a Pharisee (not even a recovering Pharisee!) who learned at the feet of Gamaliel (Acts 22:3), one of the most respected rabbis of his era. The Mishnah, a collection of oral interpretations of the Torah from around AD 200, said this about Gamaliel: "When Rabban Gamaliel the elder died, the glory of the Torah ceased, and purity and 'separateness' died." Since *Pharisee* and *separateness* share the same Hebrew root word, this comment equates the death of Gamaliel with the death of Pharisaism. This, we know, isn't true, because many Pharisees are alive and well—attending churches of various shapes and colors!

As Paul shared the Gospel in city after city, his résumé gave him instant credibility in the synagogues that supplied the foundation of the churches he planted. Not only that, but his education gave him the tools to point the church in a direction that has continued for two thousand years.

What likely motivated Paul in his educational quest? His love for God and his desire to know him better.

When Jesus was asked which of God's commandments was most important of all, he replied,

> The most important one . . . is this: "Hear, O Israel, the Lord our God, the Lord is one. Love the Lord your God with all your heart and with all your soul and with all your mind and with all your strength." The second is this: "Love your neighbor as yourself." There is no commandment greater than these.
>
> MARK 12:29–31

Notice that Jesus included the mind as a way to love God. By listing the heart, soul, mind, and strength, he was explaining that we should love God with everything that is within us.

Loving God with our mind doesn't mean we should all leave our day jobs and enroll in the nearest seminary. But it does mean that any focused intellectual study can lead us into a deeper relationship with God. This applies to the study of Scripture as well as other non-scriptural study.

The danger of intellectual pursuits, however, is that they can easily devolve into head trips that focus on anything *but* God. How many of us know people who know God's Word but somehow missed knowing God in the midst of it? The same dynamic is common in seminaries. In fact, most pastors who graduate from seminary need a few years to recover from their heady experience.

In Praise of Revelation Knowledge

At the same time, Scripture clearly tells us that to the believer, knowledge doesn't come only through what we can see and observe. Jesus promised that "the Holy Spirit, whom the Father will send in my name, will teach you all things and will remind you of everything I have said to you" (John 14:26). Jesus sent us the Holy Spirit to teach us, to reveal to us, more about him.

Detractors claim that charismatics give revelation knowledge preeminence over the Word of God. In my varied charismatic experiences, I never heard a teacher claim that revelation knowledge overrules Scripture. Kenneth Hagin once commented,

> There are no revelations outside of the Word. Any revelation
> you have that comes from the Spirit of God is in line with the
> Word of God. People get off into the devil's territory when they
> leave the Word. They say they are following the Spirit, but you
> can't follow the Holy Spirit apart from the Word.

Although no one instructed us to pursue revelation knowledge more than God's Word, we often did it anyway. Listening and acting upon the voices we hear without knowing God's Word and comparing it with our *"rhema"* word (a message from God spoken directly into our situation) places us in precarious, and at times embarrassing, situations. Emphasizing revelation knowledge over Scripture isn't necessarily evidence of Gnosticism, but it does point to Gnostic tendencies.

The Objective and Subjective Nature of Scripture

If you've ever sat in a non-charismatic Bible church worship service, you quickly realize that they give Scripture preeminence over nearly everything else. The pastor preaches an expository sermon, explaining the meaning of a passage line-by-line. People show up for Bible-based Sunday school classes in droves. Although they make no room for the exercise of "charismatic" gifts in their worship services, you know that they know Scripture and that they love God. The objective truth of God's Word guides their everyday lives.

Charismatic churches, on the other hand, offer a completely different experience. A pastor could preach a sermon based on the same Scripture passage, but the message may be completely different. The insights likely weren't gleaned from a commentary or other resources; instead, they came by the inspiration of the Holy Spirit (often through prayer and meditation). Although interested in studying Scripture, the congregation gravitates toward opportunities to exercise various "charismatic" gifts like prophecy, a word of knowledge, or healing.

Which is better? Not necessarily either one. But together, the two examples illustrate the objective and subjective nature of Scripture.

God's Word is objective truth (John 17:17). Hopefully, since the birth of the church in Acts 2, the objective message hasn't changed, although our means of expressing it has. The unchanging nature of Scripture anchors the church when culture tries to convince us to alter our values or our foundational beliefs.

Yet the Word is also a person—Jesus (John 1:1). Hebrews 4:12 tells us the Word of God is "living and active." When the Holy

Spirit reveals and applies God's objective Word to our subjective lives, we're transformed, and new life breathes into our spirits.

For years a passage in Deuteronomy may have taught you that God needed to bring the children of Israel through the wilderness in order to prepare them to enter the Promised Land. A historical, objective truth. But then one day, in the midst of a personal crisis, you read the same passage, and the Holy Spirit reveals to you that you're in the wilderness, and that God is using it to prepare you to enter a new Promised Land. A subjective truth that infuses you with hope and faith.

Which do we need most? We need both—not a balance between the two, as if we lived with 50 percent of one and 50 percent of the other. We need both at full strength.

Our leaders in the charismatic movement need solidly biblical voices to help them remain true to our historic faith and avoid straying into heresy. But those solidly biblical voices that are entrenched in the objective truth of Scripture need to loosen up, pray, and listen for the Holy Spirit's voice. Few things are as beautiful as churches and ministries anchored in the strong foundation of historically taught Scripture and that are open to the subjective ministry of the Holy Spirit.

Charismatics need to be as committed to being students of the Word as they are to following the leading of the Holy Spirit.

It's Like Flying a Kite

As I began detoxing from my whacked-out charismatic experiences, I tended to reject the subjective ministry of the Holy Spirit. I began doubting the authenticity of prophetic words and the likelihood of God's intervention into our daily lives. In the end, my faith felt cold and lifeless. Theologically correct, but spiritually bankrupt.

The relationship between the objective and subjective natures of Scripture is like flying a kite. In order for a kite to fly (the subjective nature), someone must be holding onto the string (the objective nature). The thing that keeps the kite in the air is the thing that holds it down.

New Testament worship in the early church, which models what our personal worship should look like, offered both:

> What then shall we say, brothers? When you come together, everyone has a hymn, or a word of instruction, a revelation, a tongue or an interpretation. All of these must be done for the strengthening of the church.
>
> 1 CORINTHIANS 14:26

When the body of Christ gathered, a word of instruction was shared—the objective word—as well as a revelation, a tongue, or an interpretation—a subjective word.

What is God after? Worship in spirit and in truth. Worship that is led by the Holy Spirit but also grounded in the truth of God's Word (John 4:24).

But without that objective truth, we stray into wacky theology . . . which is the subject of our next topic of study.

CHAPTER 12

If It's Strange, It Must Be of God

Wacky, Trendy Theology

Smith Wigglesworth, the great healing evangelist from the first half of the twentieth century, had an unconventional approach to healing. Because he believed praying for the sick was an act of spiritual warfare, he often punched people in their afflicted area with his fist, believing he was striking the devil.

Although Wigglesworth's unusual methods resulted in a surprising number of healings, people began describing the location of their infirmities in very general terms. Can you blame them?

At one healing service, however, Wigglesworth met his match. An Irish woman identified the area on her body in need of healing, which Wigglesworth answered with a taut punch.

Immediately, the woman drew back her fist and shouted, "Begorra, if it's a fight you want, it's a fight you'll get!" Fortunately, cooler heads prevailed and the service proceeded without further incident.

If you've been around it long enough, you know by experience that the charismatic movement attracts strange behavior, strange people, and sometimes, strange teachings. A strange and holy fire. Any time you deal with otherworldly phenomena like healing or tongues, you're going to attract a few crazies. Oftentimes, in fact, the crazies became part and parcel of the movement.

In the 1970s, we used to sing a worship chorus in church based on 1 Peter 2:9: "But ye are a chosen generation, a royal priesthood, an holy nation, a peculiar people" (KJV). We relished our identity as a peculiar people and assumed that if our behavior or the words of knowledge we received were strange, then they must be of God.

Standing on the shoulders of the great men and women who have gone before us, the strangeness continues.

Strange, but True . . .

Every few years a new charismatic phenomenon comes down the pike. Holy laughter (which we called "the joy of the Lord" in earlier years) and barking like a dog took charismatics by storm during the Toronto Blessing. A year later, the Brownsville Revival introduced us to twitching, jerking, and waving our arms in the air, yelling, "More, Lord!"

As if to up the ante, gold dust began appearing on the foreheads of worshipers and gold fillings materialized in some of their teeth. Reports circulated that feathers floated in the air in the midst of the euphoria.

Rocking back and forth, getting slain in the Spirit, repeatedly lunging forward as if some invisible being punched you in the gut, and standing with your arms in the air and waving your hands in a circular motion as if you were wafting heavenly smoke in your direction could all be interpreted as abnormal behavior by any psychologist.

But this kind of behavior doesn't exist only on the main thoroughfares of churches proclaiming that revival has come.

Everyday (ab)normal people like you and me gladly carry on the tradition.

Dancing, laughing, swaying, praying in tongues. Oh my! Outsiders would think we're crazy.

They do.

My wife, Kelley, once befriended a young woman who was on a spiritual search. Because the woman had never attended a church, Kelley invited her to join us on a Sunday morning and then prepped her on what to expect. After a forty-five minute drive from her home, the woman arrived, joined us at church, and sat with us in the second row. Kelley and I sweated bullets as we desperately hoped nothing weird would happen that morning.

Our friends welcomed the young woman, which probably calmed her nerves after venturing into this strange, new world. The opening pleasantries and announcements went without a hitch and then the worship band kicked in, rousing the congregation in worship. *Whew!* I thought. *This is going pretty well. The people raising their hands don't seem to bother her—I think this is going to work out!*

After that, the senior pastor preached a lo-o-o-ng sermon. Thirty minutes in, he announced that we were just moving out of the introduction and into the meat of his talk. Forty-five minutes after that, he began his conclusion. Although overly long, he made some salient points, and the woman seemed to be hanging in there with us.

Great! Just one more worship song and we're out of here without any weirdness.

Not so fast.

As we came to the end of the last song, a woman directly in front of us stood up and prophesied over random people in the congregation for the next twenty minutes. Kelley and I were mortified. We couldn't even muster up the courage to peek at our friend standing next to us to read the expression on her face. Do we say anything after church? Do we apologize? Do we dare ask her what she thought?

Immediately following the worship service, the woman said very little, and seeing that it was well past one o'clock, needed to get going to meet some friends.

A few days later Kelley asked the woman what she thought of her experience, and she responded with something like, "Oh, it was nice." But after that, she evaded any discussions about spiritual things. And she never returned to our church.

The apostle Paul worked hard to rein in the church at Corinth, which tended to get out of hand. During corporate worship, people were shouting out messages in tongues, prophetic words were spontaneously interrupting the sermon . . . it was a charismatic free-for-all.

Into this cavalcade of charismatic frivolity, he writes, "I thank God that I speak in tongues more than all of you. But in the church I would rather speak five intelligible words to instruct others than ten thousand words in a tongue" (1 Corinthians 14:18–19). In other words, he was saying, "I'm not against speaking in tongues. I do it all the time. But it's more important that people are encouraged by words they understand rather than mystified by a language they don't understand."

Building on this, he then explains a little further in 1 Corinthians 14:23, "So if the whole church comes together and everyone speaks in tongues, and some who do not understand or some unbelievers come in, *will they not say that you are out of your mind?*" (italics added).

As I read this, I get the distinct impression that Paul understood the effect of strange behavior on unbelievers—especially strange behavior for the sake of being strange. While not organizing corporate worship around the tastes of unbelievers, we should at least take their initial impressions into consideration.

So does that mean all peculiar behavior should be forbidden?

True, but Strange . . .

Many charismatics today, like the church in Corinth, stand on solid scriptural footing for their odd behavior.

The children of ancient Israel lived by very strict laws and practices, which set them apart from the surrounding nations. They couldn't eat pulled pork sandwiches (Leviticus 11:7); they couldn't wear clothing with a cotton/polyester blend (Leviticus 19:19); and they were forbidden from cooking a goat in its mother's milk (Exodus 23:19).

King David danced so passionately before the Lord that his wife Michal accused him of exposing himself to the young slave girls. God sided with David in the disagreement and sealed Michal's womb (2 Samuel 6).

God commanded the prophet Hosea to marry a prostitute (Hosea 1). How many pastors would bless the union of Hosea and Gomer? I sure wouldn't!

Jumping ahead into the New Testament, we read about John the Baptist—the greatest of all the prophets—who lived in the wilderness, feasting on locusts and honey.

Agabus tied a belt around his hands and feet and prophesied that Paul would be bound in a similar fashion if he returned to Jerusalem (Acts 21).

But the prophet Ezekiel was the poster child of weirdness. God called him to create a miniature replica of Jerusalem, then lay next to it on one side of his body for 390 days and then lay on his other side another forty days.

But that's not the end of the strangeness. God then called Ezekiel to cook his meals over a fire of human waste. With a little persuasion, Ezekiel convinced God to let him cook his meals over cow dung instead (such a deal—read about it in Ezekiel 4).

Then God told him to shave his hair and beard, and separate it into thirds. With one third of the hair, God instructed him to perform a public burning in Jerusalem. With another third, he was told to walk around the city, throw some hair on the ground, and strike it with his sword. Last of all, God commanded him to toss the remaining third into the wind (Ezekiel 5). The man must have been blessed with a full head of hair.

But for the coup de grace, God called Isaiah to walk the streets of Jerusalem naked and unashamed for three years (Isaiah 20).

What does this tell us? Odd behavior in the Bible was common enough that it almost wouldn't be considered strange.

To Be or Not to Be (Strange)—That Is the Question!

So does that mean we're all supposed to trade in our everyday clothes for white robes, practice that faraway look in our eyes, hone our sign-making skills, and march around town portending the end of the age?

Of course not.

In the vast majority of examples in Scripture, God commanded *his prophets* to act strangely—not a church or even a home fellowship group. The prophet's odd behavior was symbolic and provided a contrast to the normal behavior of the prophet and the rest of the people.

At times God may ask us to behave in unconventional ways, but bizarre behavior is by far the exception, not the rule. Exuberant worship pleases God, but strange worship often ceases being worship because it draws attention to us.

Revelation Knowledge or Revelation Misinformation?

Of far more concern to me in the charismatic movement is our penchant for strange theology. Many charismatics have an insatiable appetite for a "fresh word"—something that no one has said before. We want the strange, the novel teaching. What does insisting on a "fresh word" imply about the Word God has already given us?

I wonder if some charismatics get so bored with the gospel that they need something else to hold their attention.

Over the years various "peculiar" theologies have titillated the minds of charismatics:

- Christians are "little gods"

- Our words "create"

- All authority has been given to us to preach the gospel

- Each person of the Trinity is composed of another smaller trinity

- We must "pay the price" for the anointing

- The anointing comes in various shapes and sizes (e.g., the leper's anointing, the priestly anointing, the kingly anointing)

- Jesus was the first "born-again man"

- Jesus paid our debt in hell

While believing some of these teachings wouldn't doom a person to hell, they either give us a faulty impression of ourselves, Jesus, or the cross. But when we confuse our authority with Christ's, or we diminish the price he paid for us on the cross, we stray into a different gospel. Paul admonished the church in Corinth:

> I am astonished that you are so quickly deserting the one who called you by the grace of Christ and are turning to a different gospel—which is really no gospel at all. Evidently some people are throwing you into confusion and are trying to pervert the gospel of Christ. But even if we or an angel from heaven should preach a gospel other than the one we preached to you, let him be eternally condemned!
>
> GALATIANS 1:6–8

The last sentence in this passage really jumps out at me. Paul is saying, "If you're hearing a *new* teaching, it's not from God."

The charismatic movement has long esteemed the *rhema* word over the *logos* word. For decades, charismatic Bible teachers distinguished the difference between the two Greek words, proclaiming that a fresh *rhema* word is a message from God spoken directly into your situation. The *logos* word, on the other hand, is the unchanging Word of God.

Bible teachers who focus primarily on the *rhema* word often develop viewpoints on Scripture that no one has ever heard before—kind of like some of the teachings I just mentioned. Bible teachers who primarily focus on the *logos* word build their beliefs on the historically interpreted, unchanging Word of God. This is a bit of an overstatement, but you get the idea.

But get this: *Logos* and *rhema* are virtually interchangeable. Any Greek scholar worth his or her salt will tell you that the distinction our favorite charismatic Bible teachers make between the two simply doesn't exist.

For example, Hebrews 11:3 tells us, "By faith we understand that the worlds were prepared by the word of God" (NASB). The Greek translation for *word* in this passage is *rhema*. However, we read in 2 Peter 3:5 that "by the word of God the heavens existed long ago" (NASB). Both passages say basically the same thing, except this second reference to *word* uses the Greek word *logos*.

Why do these "rhema" teachers insist on differentiating between the two? Because it allows them to develop their own homespun beliefs without being held scripturally accountable for what they teach. I'm not the Holy Spirit, so I can't read their hearts, but that's the best answer I can come up with.

Who can question a rhema word when it arrived via a direct pipeline from heaven? Chances are that person heard about the teaching in question from somebody else, and because they never formally studied theology or the Greek language for themselves (check their credentials), they believed it as fact.

The writer of Hebrews warns, "Do not be carried away by all kinds of strange teachings" (13:9). The word for *strange* in this verse means "foreign" or "novel." When I participated in the charismatic mainstream, all too often we snacked on the junk food of new teachings while ignoring the healthy staples of the Christian diet, like love, repentance, holy living, the cross, and most of all, Jesus. And besides, why would God allow the church to miss the boat for two thousand years concerning a host of new, important teachings?

Not to bore you with the meanings of Greek words, but the word *peculiar*—as in "peculiar people"—from 1 Peter 2:9 (KJV), might provide a little clarity to this discussion. When the word was first incorporated in the King James Version, it didn't mean "strange." It's actually a Middle English word meaning "personal" or "purchased," as in personal property. Newer translations offer a completely different rendition from the King's English: "a people belonging to God" or "a people for his own possession." We have been chosen, as people belonging to God, to declare the praises of our King. When our behavior or teachings draw attention to ourselves or away from Jesus, we cease living up to our high calling from heaven.

As I wrap up this discussion, let me leave you with a few concluding thoughts: Scripture never offers strangeness as a quality to pursue or a value to uphold. Sometimes God instructs individuals (as opposed to groups) to engage in strange behavior as a symbolic action, usually directed at other believers. But strangeness should never serve as a sign of God's presence or direction.

More important, strange and novel teachings that can't be supported by the obvious meaning of Scripture, as well as a majority view in the history of the church, are likely heretical. Don't get burned by the strange fire of this kind.

If in the past you have bought into strange behavior or strange teachings and now you regret it, laugh at yourself. Laughter is good medicine. Then make amends with those you've hurt and share a good laugh. Welcome to the club. Lastly, let it motivate you to become a more dedicated student of God's Word and a more ardent worshiper of Jesus.

The Word of God is living and active because the Word of God is a person—Jesus. Unfortunately, we often treat him like a formula or principle instead.

CHAPTER 13

Give Me a Principle, Not a Personal God

An Assessment of the Word of Faith Movement

If you've hung around the charismatic movement very long or you watch Christian television, you can probably repeat the following Bible verses in your sleep:

> Beloved, I wish above all things that thou mayest prosper and be in health, even as thy soul prospereth. (3 John 2 KJV)

> "Bring all the tithes into the storehouse, that there may be food in My house, and try Me now in this," says the Lord of hosts, "If I will not open for you the windows of heaven and pour out for you such blessing that there will not be room enough to receive it." (Malachi 3:10 NKJV)

> And you shall remember the Lord your God, for it is He who gives you power to get wealth. (Deuteronomy 8:18 NKJV)

Like Pippin, the ravenous hobbit in *The Lord of the Rings* book and movie series, who enjoyed first breakfast and second breakfast, many charismatic churches serve up a generous helping of "first sermon" and "second sermon." Every week believers around the globe listen intently to the "second sermon" in church. In non-charismatic churches, "second sermon" would be classified as the only sermon. It usually follows the offering—a special music rendition on the organ (for our traditional friends) or a poignant solo from someone on the worship team (for our hip, seeker-friendly evangelical friends).

In the 1980s, however, charismatics bumped the only sermon into "second sermon" position and introduced a "first sermon." Usually between the extended praise and worship segment of the service (singing) and the offering, the senior pastor stands and offers the new "first sermon." This sermon is intended to inspire—but sometimes browbeat—the congregation into giving generously. It also provides people with extra time to write their checks so the offering can move along quickly before "second sermon" commences. On certain occasions, usually during a financial crunch at church, the "first sermon" can last longer than the "second sermon."

"We will now receive the Lord's tithe and our offering," the pastor begins. In rowdier churches, at this point the people clap or even stand to their feet. If Las Vegas odds makers attended the church, they would say the odds are about 50 percent that one of the aforementioned verses would then serve as the text of the "first sermon." Back in the day, the pastor asked people to pull out the largest bill in their wallet or purse and then hold it up to God while they prayed. But since people nowadays forgo cash, opting for debit cards, credit cards, or checks, the practice has more or less ceased.

During the prayer over the offering, the pastor usually implores, "God, we plant this seed into your fields and believe that you will return a hundredfold increase into our laps—pressed down, shaken together, running out all over." Pastors with lesser faith only demand a tenfold increase. At the conclusion of the prayer, the offering is received, followed by the "second sermon."

Why do so many charismatic churches employ an additional sermon? Because their pastors sincerely believe that when their people give, God will return their gifts back to them . . . with interest. Not so ironically, the addition of an extra sermon in corporate worship also coincides with the expansion of the Word of Faith or prosperity movement.

What's in a Name?

The Word of Faith movement goes by a variety of names: Word-Faith, prosperity gospel, health and wealth. I've always preferred the more derisive terms:

- Name it and claim it
- Believe it and receive it
- Confess it and possess it
- Blab it and grab it
- Fake it and jake it (actually, I made up this one!)

Although outsiders may see them as one and the same, the charismatic movement and Word of Faith movement differ from each other but peacefully coexist. Thirty years ago the Word of Faith movement subsisted as a minority viewpoint within the charismatic movement. But in recent years they have begun to overlap to the point that they appear virtually the same.

The reason for their gradual but imminent marriage isn't difficult to discern—most of the leaders who speak on behalf of charismatics also happen to be Word of Faith teachers. Oh yeah, and they also operate their own television ministries. Whoever controls the airwaves calls the agenda.

Charismatics believe that the Holy Spirit operates in the same way that he did in the New Testament church. The Holy Spirit endues the body of Christ with power so we can do the stuff—heal, multiply the loaves and fishes, work miracles, even pull coins out of the mouths of fishes—just like Jesus.

The Word of Faith movement codifies that belief into a principle or law. Charismatics believe God has the power to heal. Word of Faith people believe God wants everyone healed . . . now!

Charismatics believe God *can* multiply back to you the financial gifts you invest into his kingdom. Word of Faith people believe God *will* multiply back to you the gifts you invest into his kingdom.

Charismatics believe God *can* help you get that job over the other six applicants. Word of Faith people believe God *will* get you that job. Just find the Scripture that applies to your need and fervently repeat it until God answers your prayer. Granted, that's a bit of an oversimplification, but it's the general idea.

Word of Faith teachers tell us that God has arranged divine principles that govern the universe. If you give, God will give back to you in greater measure. You overcome sickness by confessing that by Jesus' stripes you are healed (Isaiah 53:5). If you can't find a parking space, you pray, "Dear Lord Jesus, full of mercy and grace, please find me a parking space!"

The Word of Faith movement has even gone mainstream evangelical. People who don't even pray in tongues proclaim that if we pray the prayer of Jabez, and really believe it, then God will grant our request (if you didn't read the book, you can find the passage in 1 Chronicles 4:10). Don't let the fact that Jesus never prayed this prayer, or that his heavenly Father didn't keep Jesus from pain, or that Jabez's prayer is mentioned only once in Scripture, prevent you from repeating this mantra . . . I mean, standing on this prayer.

Not That It's *All* Bad

Before we intoxicate ourselves with our own arrogance, let's get this on the table: Given the choice, we all prefer to be rich. Go ahead, admit it. If someone on the street offered you ten million dollars, would you take it? Absolutely. I would.

Secondly, despite the many times prosperity teachers tried to cram their teachings down my throat—and I willingly swallowed a few times—I'd have to say that not all of it was lethal.

The prosperity movement taught me not only that God can bless me and that God *is able* to bless me, but that he *wants* to bless me. All too often, Christians assume God only blessed people in the Bible. God promised to bless Abraham, and he died a very wealthy man. Isaac and Jacob met a similar fate as their forefather. And after a few bumps in the road, Joseph met with quite a bit of success.

Abraham believed that God would bless him with many descendants—at that time a sure sign of financial security—and it was credited to him as righteousness (Genesis 15:6; Romans 4:3).

At times I have planted seeds out of my need, and to my amazement, I reaped a harvest. Sometimes fivefold. Sometimes tenfold. I'm still waiting for the hundredfold return we used to believe God for at church.

Too often we expect too little from God—and God lives down to our expectations. Believing that God can intervene in our lives, even our finances, is called hope. Without it, the heart grows sick.

For this, recovering charismatics can be grateful.

Blessing Is More Than Throwing Money at Our Problems

All too often we define blessing from our perspective rather than God's. What does blessing look like from my point of view? Perhaps that ten-million-dollar gift I mentioned earlier, or a new Jeep Wrangler I can drive through the Rocky Mountains. Most people—Americans at least—would define blessing as the accumulation of lots of stuff and the elimination of pain. It would take lots of persuasion to convince me that this doesn't resemble the Word of Faith movement or the prosperity gospel.

The God I know, however, doesn't seem as enamored with accumulating stuff and avoiding pain. He gave us his only Son, who then suffered a painful death on the cross. The upside-down kingdom at work.

What does blessing look like from God's perspective? A new or renewed relationship with him. A restored marriage. In fact, pain and hardship often accompany blessings of this kind. The greatest breakthroughs in my relationship with Jesus occurred in the midst of pain or loss. My marriage didn't turn the corner until my wife and I experienced some very painful moments, which propelled us closer to each other.

Unhealthy parents who care little about their children give them everything they want in the hopes of helping them avoid suffering. Insistent children who get everything they want usually become spoiled brats who grow into very broken adults. You can't throw money at a problem and call it a blessing.

Getting Personal About Prosperity

Years ago I dabbled in the Word of Faith movement. I enjoyed listening to down-to-earth teachers like Kenneth Hagin and Kenneth Copeland. Kenneth Hagin, in fact, taught me to believe that God can really do anything. But over time a nagging feeling began to grow inside that something was missing. I realized that these well-intentioned men had reduced—or better yet, depersonalized—God into a principle. In the Word of Faith movement, we never asked God to reveal his will. We decided his will for ourselves and then expected God to answer our prayers. In fact, we were taught that the ultimate "faith killer" in prayer was the phrase, "God, if it's your will . . ." Perhaps we didn't want to know his will because it didn't agree with ours, so we decided to stop asking him and start telling him (or is that "demanding" of him?) what we wanted.

"The secret to getting the desires of your heart," we were told, "is to tap into the divine principles God has established to govern the universe." These divine principles include:

- When you give, God will return it back to you tenfold or a hundredfold.

- We have what we say, so we must speak our desires into existence.

- God's Word never returns void, so keep on confessing God's Word over your situation until he answers your prayer.

- If God promises prosperity to you in his Word, you can hold him to his promise.

The problem with a faith built on principles is that it leaves little room for a relationship with a personal God. The universe can't run on both principles and a personal God. A personal God cannot be easily explained and often acts outside of our expectations of him. He may define justice, compassion, and healing differently than we do. His priorities may—and often do—look much different than ours. Most important, serving an impersonal God robs us of the satisfaction that comes from growing in an intimate relationship with him. He simply becomes a means to getting what we want.

A faith built on principles offers little interaction with God. God sets up the world with a specific number of principles and then allows the world to be governed by those principles. In reality, the prosperity movement is nothing more than a charismatic version of deism.

The *Merriam-Webster Dictionary* defines deism as "a movement or system of thought advocating natural religion, emphasizing morality, and in the eighteenth century denying the interference of the Creator with the laws of the universe." Did you catch that last part? Deists believe the Creator of the universe establishes laws that govern it, and then he refuses to interfere with his creation. When we're told that we need to have "faith in our faith" (which cannot be advocated in Scripture) rather than "faith in God" (which is advocated in Scripture), we know we're being sold a bill of goods.

If I didn't know better, I would think that some people in the Word of Faith movement were simply charismatic Christian Scientists!

When we worship a deistic God rather than a personal God, we don't have to answer for our materialistic pursuits. In fact, a deistic faith calls into question who it is that is ultimately in control. Is it God who establishes the divine principles, or the people who confess them into existence?

Before moving on, this question merits a little more exploration. . . .

CHAPTER 14

I Think I'm Catching a Cold . . . Oops, I Mean a Healing

The Secret to Positive Confession

How would your life be different if you were God? Laying aside all platitudes like bringing peace on earth or reversing the polarity of the caloric universe so that every food substance consisting of cheese or chocolate was fat-free and salads were deathly lethal—how would you alter your life?

Few books have taken the reading public by storm like the recent book *The Secret*. With appearances on *Larry King Live* and *Oprah*, author Rhonda Byrne has sold millions of copies of her self-help book.

And who gets the credit for her overwhelming sales? She does, because she envisioned her success into existence. Through the Law of Attraction, she writes, "There isn't a single thing that you cannot do. . . . [The Law of Attraction] can give you whatever you want." By it "you will come to know how you can have, be, or do anything you want." The product description on the DVD version claims, "This is The Secret to everything—the secret to unlimited joy, health, money, relationships, love, youth: everything you have ever wanted."

Wow—that's a pretty big secret!

The Law of Attraction, she explains in her book, rests on a universal truth that the thoughts we choose to think and the ideas we choose to believe determine the destiny of our lives, good or bad. By intentionally choosing specific thoughts and beliefs regarding our success, we attract that particular area of success into our lives.

Byrne reiterates the Law of Attraction in various ways:

- "Nothing [good or bad] can come into your experience unless you summon it through persistent thoughts."
- "Your thoughts are the primary cause of everything."
- "Your current reality or your current life is a result of the thoughts you have been thinking."

The Secret to Positive Confession

Recently I viewed an extensive segment of *The Secret* DVD. Watching the video, something deep inside me started getting excited. The promises of wealth, success, and fulfilling relationships really appealed to me. *Maybe they're right*, I thought. *I need to watch what I say and stop exposing myself to anything negative, painful, or unfulfilling.* The video mesmerized me like some televangelists mesmerize me when they tell me I can have whatever I say.

Intersperse the material with a few Bible verses and remove all the New Age-y terminology and you'd think you were reading a book or watching a video about positive confession.

The positive confession movement isn't really a movement at all. It's simply a substratum layer that lies at the foundation of

Word of Faith theology. However, it has so permeated charismatic faith and practice that it bears further assessment.

In the beginning, God created the heavens and the earth with a word: "Let there be," as in "Let there be light." In Hebrew, the word is *hayah*. Building on this foundational premise, Word of Faith teachers instruct us that because we are created in the image of God, we create with our words, as well. Because "we have what we say," we better watch what we say. If we speak negativity, sickness, poverty, or doubt *over* our lives, we'll suffer negativity, sickness, poverty, or doubt *in* our lives. On the other hand, if we speak positivity, health, wealth, and faith, we'll reap more of the same.

Because "the tongue has the power of life and death" (Proverbs 18:21), we must be careful what we say. Here's a little reminder of what, and what not, to say, in case you get stuck in an elevator with someone from the Word of Faith movement:

Don't Say . . .	Say . . .
"I think I'm catching a cold."	"I think I'm catching a healing."
"You make me sick."	"You're a blessing to me."
"I was just laid off from work."	"God is positioning me for a fulfilling job that pays me more money than I ever dreamed."
"We're going under."	"We're going over."
"I'm broke."	"Thank God, I'm rich!"

At church we sang songs about the life of God in us. We have his life, his nature, his ability. And every morning when we wake up, we were told to repeat to ourselves something to this effect:

I'm blessed going in, blessed going out, blessed in the city, blessed in the fields. I'm the head not the tail, above not beneath. I'm the top, not the bottom. I am the child of God, and the favor of God rests on me.

Interestingly enough, this mantra wasn't really a prayer because it wasn't addressed to God—it was addressed to the heavenlies so that all creation, as well as the powers of good and the forces of evil, could hear us.

If you search for some of the phrases on the Internet from the above mantra, you probably won't be surprised that many of them appear on Web sites that make no mention of being Christian. In fact, many of those sites extol the virtues of *The Secret*.

Really, this should come as no surprise, because Rhonda Byrne and the progenitor of the Word of Faith movement studied at the same school. Well, kind of.

When she wrote *The Secret*, Rhonda Byrne admittedly borrowed heavily from *The Science of Getting Rich*, a book penned by Wallace Wattles in 1910. Wattles studied New Thought philosophy and contributed articles to a magazine based on its teachings. A year before he died, he released his book. Many of Byrne's colleagues, who contribute to *The Secret* DVD (which differs from the book but reiterates its teachings), openly confess that their teachings are based on New Thought, as well.

E. W. Kenyon, whose writings heavily influenced Kenneth Hagin, the "granddaddy" of the Word of Faith movement, was educated at Emerson College, a hotbed of New Thought. He eventually became a pastor and an author whose writings line the bookshelves of virtually every Word of Faith teacher.

The men were born about the same time—Wattles in 1860 and Kenyon in 1867—although Wattles died prematurely in 1910. No evidence exists that the men knew each other, although they thrived in New Thought teaching about the same time.

What is the "theology" of New Thought? Just read *The Secret* and you'll know. You can have whatever you want if you envision it. Kenyon's addition of "positive confession" parallels this belief.

The Positive in Positive Confession

Linking E. W. Kenyon with New Thought works many Christian apologists into a dither. And most make a wholesale rejection of positive confession.

But is there power in our words? Absolutely!

Nobody likes to hang around negative people. People who view the world from a glass-half-empty perspective drag everybody down with them. And we all know it rubs off on us.

Early in our marriage, my mother-in-law scolded Kelley and me because we were overly negative with each other. "Watch what you say," she lectured us. And she was right. After changing the way we spoke with each another, our marriage surprisingly improved.

To an extent, our words are performative. In other words, our words affect certain outcomes in our lives. If you tell your daughter that she'll never amount to anything, the chances are much greater than average that she'll grow up believing she's a failure. If I look at myself in the mirror every day and say, "You're an idiot," eventually my words will sink in.

Dr. Masaru Emoto, a researcher in Japan, conducted experiments on the relationship between words and thoughts in the formation of water crystals.

He began by drawing polluted water from the Fujiwara Dam. After freezing a specimen on a Petri dish, he examined the water crystal under a microscope and observed that it took on no particular molecular structure. But in a separate Petri dish, he prayed a blessing over the murky water, froze it, and crystals appeared as ornate as those formed from pristine spring waters in Japan.

Next, he printed positive and negative messages, taped them to bottles of distilled water, and then froze them overnight. Crystals grown in bottles with written messages like "Love and Appreciation" and "Thank you" taped on the outside resulted in beautiful, translucent, complex structures.

But the sample from the bottle with the message "Adolf Hitler" resulted in very under-formed crystals. Interestingly enough, the message "You make me sick, I will kill you" written on the side resulted in no crystal formation at all. Praying for the water from a different location affected the results of crystal formation just as dramatically—regardless of distance.

His further studies demonstrated that spoken words resulted in the same outcome. Dr. Emoto, a Buddhist, comments:

> This principle is what I think makes swearing and slang words destructive. These words are not in accordance with the laws of nature. So, for example, I think you would probably find higher rates of violent crime in areas where a lot of negative language is being used. Just as the Bible says, first there was the Word, and God created all of Creation from the Word.[1]

Scripture bears out Dr. Emoto's premise. When you "confess with your mouth, 'Jesus is Lord,' and believe in your heart that God raised him from the dead, you will be saved" (Romans 10:9). Your verbal confession carries spiritual and eternal implications and changes.

We also read that at the name of Jesus every knee should bow and every tongue confess that Jesus Christ is Lord (Philippians 2:10–11). In the Hebrew understanding, invoking the name of Jesus meant invoking his manifest presence.

The key question here is who—or what—are we invoking?

Our Confessions Reveal Our Hearts

"Out of the abundance of the heart the mouth speaks," Jesus explained in Matthew 12:34 (ESV). The words we speak, the confessions we make, reflect our truest values. Our words betray our heart.

As I said before, watching *The Secret* DVD mesmerized me in the same way that the promises of certain Word of Faith teachers mesmerize me. I can have everything I want: Wealth. A good job. A fulfilling relationship. Stuff—lots of stuff. All I must do is think the right thoughts and say the right words.

Is God's purpose for my life to prove to the world that Christians should be the richest people on earth? Paul wrote,

> But godliness with contentment is great gain. For we brought nothing into the world, and we can take nothing out of it. But if we have food and clothing, we will be content with that. People who want to get rich fall into temptation and a trap and into many foolish and harmful desires that plunge men into ruin and destruction.
>
> 1 TIMOTHY 6:6–9

What does God want for me? Godliness with contentment. The desire for riches ensnares me in a web of ruin and destruction. The ruin and destruction may involve finances or relationships, but ultimately, it involves my relationship with Jesus.

Positive confession, like *The Secret*, offers people a means of pursuing the desires of their flesh. Paul warned us about people of this sort: "They exchanged the truth of God for a lie, and worshiped and served created things rather than the Creator" (Romans 1:25). The things of this world will never satisfy. They promise us happiness, but once we attain them, we want more. By focusing our lives on getting what we want, we exchange the truth of a relationship with a loving God for an idol of our own choosing. Even the deep desire for fulfilling relationships can become idolatrous.

All too often, our "confessions" reveal that we set our sights way too low. Our dreams are too small. Instead of desiring the Creator, we opt for his creation. God doesn't expect every Christian to live in poverty, but he does want every Christian to find their contentment in him. To find security only in him. To hang onto the things of this world loosely. And to make him our sole desire.

The Negative in Positive Confession

Most of the positive confessions I've spoken or heard were nothing more than a formula. God played a minimal role when I spoke to the heavenlies. Except, of course, when I reminded him of his promises to bless me with riches or good health, as if he needed reminding.

But if God controls the universe with divine principles, and my words create, all I need to do is find the right formula, and I can make him do whatever I want.

- If I can just get enough people praying . . .
- If I just stop sinning . . .
- If I just start reading the Bible more . . .
- If I just use the right words . . .
- If I just stop speaking negative confessions . . .

. . . then I can make God do what I want him to do.

There's another word for formula: superstition. If it worked for another person, it should work for me.

My flesh loves formulas because my faith resides in the formula, which I can control, and not in a personal God, whom I can't control. Formulas leave no room for mystery or for God to act outside my plans.

Really, placing my faith in a formula—in charismatic terms, having "faith in your faith"—rather than in a personal God, reveals my fear of not being in control.

Control is nothing more than an illusion. When life goes according to my plans, I begin to believe that I'm in control. At that point, my plans may be following God's plans out of sheer coincidence (or make that a God-cidence if you're watching your confession). But when life takes an unplanned direction change that doesn't follow my desires, I feel out of control.

My attraction to positive confession results from three attributes of God that I continually wrestle with:

- God is good
- God is all-wise
- God is all-powerful

Does God always act in my best interests? Does he know better than me what is best for me? Is God truly in control of my life's outcome? If I answer yes to all three questions, then I cannot place my trust in the confession of my mouth, and I'm not in control.

But God *is* good. Romans 8:28 tells us that "in all things God works for the good of those who love him." Regardless of how tenuous or stress-free our lives, God can only do good to those who love him. Looking back, I feel embarrassed by my attempts to hold God to his Word—as if he weren't good, as if he weren't faithful.

But God *is* all-wise. God knows what's better for me than I do because his ways and his thoughts are higher than mine (Isaiah 55:9). As much as I dislike hardship and pain, I learn more from them than from any success I might experience. Besides, how can we know what's best for us with hearts as deceitful as ours (Jeremiah 17:9)?

And God *is* all-powerful. The psalmist wrote, "Our God is in heaven; he does whatever pleases him" (Psalm 115:3). Wouldn't you love to do whatever you want, whenever you want? Just once, wouldn't you like to drink directly out of the milk jug or rest your feet on the coffee table? You might not be able to do whatever you want, but God can. That's what makes him God!

God loves us, he knows what he's doing, and he's in control.

Word of Faith teachers tell us that our words create because we are created in God's image—we're God's children . . . little gods. Little or big, a god is a god. Either we are or we aren't. If we're little gods, we don't need God's wisdom to make decisions.

If we're little gods, we don't need anyone to save us and we don't need Jesus. If Jesus' disciples were little gods, then they should, and will, get whatever they want. Yet Jesus taught them to pray, "Your kingdom come, your will be done" (Matthew 6:10).

The desire to be like God began in the garden of Eden, when the serpent tempted Adam and Eve.

> "You will not surely die," the serpent said to the woman. "For God knows that when you eat of it your eyes will be opened, *and you will be like God*, knowing good and evil."
>
> GENESIS 3:4–5 (ITALICS ADDED)

Our sinful nature tells us that we can be like God. *The Secret* tells us we can be like God. But in the end, our fleshly desires remind us how far from God we really are.

It's More Than a River That Runs Through Egypt

A few years ago the father of a friend of mine was brutally murdered. When I heard the news, I phoned my friend to express my sorrow and concern.

"Actually, I'm fine," he told me. "We refuse to give Satan any satisfaction in taking my father's life. So we're just fine."

"It's okay to feel the loss of your father," I reassured him, with tears streaming down my cheeks. "Was it hard to bury him?"

"Well, we're sad to see him go, and we're going to miss him, but I can't say it's really bothering me. Rather than feel discouraged, we felt like it was more important to get back to the ministry God has called us to."

I was flabbergasted. Nobody in the family allowed themselves to feel the pain of the loss of this man of God. Since two or three months had passed since the murder, the initial shock had likely worn off.

Positive confession often serves as the pretty wrapping paper on a package called denial. If you really believe in positive confession, you refuse to acknowledge reality if it doesn't align with your will.

A well-known charismatic leader wrote a monthly column for a charismatic publication. While still middle-aged, he was stricken with cancer but refused to share his physical challenges with his readers or the people in his church community. He eventually died a premature death, while his relatives insisted he died of natural causes.

In my experience, well-intended believers have denied the reality of their sicknesses, sick marriages, broken marriages, financial devastations, deep feelings of discouragement, lapses in employment, and concern for the salvation of their children. To these people, expressing sorrow or pain or disappointment is admitting defeat, which to them is akin to compromising with the enemy.

Scripture, on the other hand, affirms the full range of emotions.

Over a third of the psalms are laments, poems acknowledging pain, suffering, betrayal, discouragement, and loneliness.

When King Jehoshaphat was told that a mighty army was mobilizing to attack, he acknowledged the reality of his situation openly before the people of Judah. And God spared them (2 Chronicles 20).

Paul confessed that he boasted in his weakness—boasted!—so that Christ's power could rest on him. "That is why, for Christ's sake, I delight in weaknesses, in insults, in hardships, in persecutions, in difficulties. For when I am weak, then I am strong" (2 Corinthians 12:10). How can we truly be strong if we can't admit our weaknesses?

Most significant of all are Jesus' words in the garden of Gethsemane the night before he was nailed to the cross. Acknowledging the pain that lay ahead, he asked God to remove the cup of suffering. Jesus wanted to die for our sins, but he didn't want to endure the cross. Nevertheless he prayed, "Not my will, but yours be done" (Luke 22:42).

Burying our feelings doesn't mean they go away. They simply grow roots so deep and strong that when the feelings surface again, they turn into anger, bitterness, discouragement, and sometimes depression. The longer we live in denial, the more difficult it is to remove those roots from our lives. Voicing our feelings and the reality of our situation reminds us of who we are and who God is. This in turn places us in a posture to receive.

In recent chapters we've looked at prosperity and positive confession, but what about healing? Does God still heal, and is it okay to expect him to heal us?

CHAPTER 15

Is All Sickness From the Devil?

Healing and God's Will

The church I attended as a child did "the stuff." It was a hotspot of the Jesus People Movement—a legitimately powerful move of the Holy Spirit in the 1970s. Throngs of young men with no shirts and ragged jeans and their girlfriends in short shorts and halter tops gave their hearts to Jesus.

Every Sunday night at church, people waited in long lines to be baptized. Most were hippies who hadn't taken a shower in a while, so sometimes the water in the baptistery became so dirty that it had to be drained and refilled again in the middle of the baptism service. Nobody led the singing; different people in the congregation spontaneously led out in a chorus and everyone else followed along.

One Sunday night, however, became a defining moment in my life. A man in a wheelchair who had been attending our church decided that he wanted to be baptized. As a seven- or eight-year-old, I didn't know if he was a paraplegic or confined to his wheelchair because of some other debilitating condition. All I knew was that I had never seen him walk.

That night, when it was his turn, he was lifted out of his wheelchair and carried into the baptistery at the front of the sanctuary. He shared with the packed church why he wanted to be baptized and then was lowered into the water.

Suddenly the man came shooting out of the tank, jumping up and down and splashing everyone around him. "I'm healed! I can walk!" he cried out. Erupting in applause, the congregation rose to their feet and gave God a clap offering. I remember the experience particularly well because I sat in the front row and the man splashing in the water not only made me wet, but he made my coloring book wet, too.

After about ten minutes of clapping and praising God, the baptisms continued where they had left off, and the evening worship service continued. Business as usual. Just another night at church.

For years I questioned whether I had exaggerated the events, like many children do. But thirty years later I bumped into Kent Verbal, my best friend when I was a child, who had sat next to me at that same church service.

"Mike, do you remember that man in the wheelchair who was baptized at church and God healed him?" I hadn't even mentioned the event. Kent continued, "We were sitting in the front row at church and he splashed the water so much that he got us wet!" Amazingly enough, our recollections of the event were identical.

If tongues (at least the affirmation of its existence) serve as the litmus test of a true-blue charismatic, then a firm belief in healing must run a close second. The precursors to the charismatic movement were teachers and preachers who advocated healing—many out of the holiness movements of the late 1800s. Men like A. B. Simpson and Alexander Dowie tilled the soil for the Pentecostal harvest in the early 1900s, which paved the way for modern-day charismatics.

Full of Faith and Empty Promises

Delving into the ministry of healing is quite precarious. Do we demonstrate our faith by proclaiming that God *will* heal? Or do we give doubt room to flourish by qualifying our prayers with "If it's your will, Lord"?

Based on what we hear from some teachers, you'd think every believer should live sick-free practically forever. Never a head cold. Never a case of the flu. And especially never a stomach virus—not to mention arthritis, cancer, or heart disease. Every sanctified, blood-bought, spirit-filled, faith-confessing believer should die from old age, at around one hundred years. Besides, the Word of God tells us that by his stripes, "you were"—not *will be*—"healed" (1 Peter 2:24 NKJV).

When I was a senior in college, I served as the head chaplain in a dorm of around two hundred men. Someone asked me to pray for another man in my building whose mother was deathly sick with cancer. I issued a call throughout the dorm for the men to pray. Later that night, around twenty men showed up, including the young man whose mother was sick, and we spent the next hour or so in heartfelt prayer. With great fervency we confessed every Scripture we could remember that mentions healing. We bound the powers of darkness and cursed the cancer. Adam, the young man with the sick mother, sat silently.

At the conclusion of the meeting, I exhorted the men, "We just need to *pray through* until Adam's mom is healed."

"What do you mean by 'pray through'?" Adam asked me afterward.

"You know, keep praying until God heals her."

I was certain God was going to heal her, especially because the whole Oral Roberts University campus was praying for her, as well. I mean, if God can't work through the corporate prayers of a university founded by a healing evangelist, could he even heal at all?

A few days later, Adam's mother died. We did everything right. We prayed fervently, spoke the Word over her, called the "things that are not as though they were" (Romans 4:17) . . . yet she died.

Later I heard that Adam asked his wing chaplain, "If Mike said all we need to do is 'pray through,' and we prayed through, then why did she die?" My heart aches remembering the situation.

Does All Sickness Come From Satan?

Few events shake us like being told a loved one is healed, and we believe it, even depend on it, yet our loved one dies. It can rattle the faith of even the strongest Christian.

As a pastor, more people than I can count have asked me, with tears in their eyes, "Why did God let my brother die? Why didn't he heal him? We prayed and prayed. We believed that God would raise him out of his bed, but God did nothing!"

Earlier in my life, if I got sick, I assumed that somehow I must have given Satan an entryway into my life. I must have sinned or at least spoken a negative confession that gave Satan permission to attack me. In order to overcome my sickness, I needed to take authority over the powers of darkness that were coming against me. Rather than give in to the sickness, I needed to live as if it didn't exist.

Is all sickness a spiritual attack? Should everyone be healed when we pray for them? Should every true believer die of old age?

Healing formed a major thrust of Jesus' ministry. I say a major thrust because proclaiming the coming kingdom was *the* major thrust. Healing, raising the dead, cleansing lepers, driving out demons—along with preaching and teaching—all served as different ways to usher in the kingdom of heaven on earth (Matthew 10:7–8).

The Gospels give an account of at least thirty healings that Jesus performed. Dr. Ronald Kydd, a seminary professor at Tyndale

Seminary in Toronto, comments that "if one focuses on the part of the gospel of Mark that deals only with the ministry of Jesus—that is, excluding the accounts of the passion and resurrection—a full 47 percent of the material is devoted to Christ's healing ministry."[1]

When I study the relationship between Jesus' deliverance ministry and healing ministry—again, both kingdom ministries—here is what I find:

1. **Deliverance played a significant role in Jesus' ministry.** The words *demons, devil, Satan, unclean spirits,* and *evil spirits* appear 117 times in the Gospels. Non-charismatics and recovering charismatics often try to avoid the "embarrassing" prevalence of demonic activity in Jesus' ministry. But regardless of our bending, twisting, and rationalizing, it's in the Bible in black and white . . . and red letters.

2. **Demonization was considered a sickness.** Various passages in the Gospels list the infirmities that Jesus healed in other people, which included sicknesses and demonization. One man brought to Jesus his son, who was suffering from seizures. We then read that "Jesus rebuked the demon, and it came out of the boy, and he was healed from that moment" (Matthew 17:18). Jesus healed people of their demonic infirmities in the same way that he healed people of their physical infirmities.

3. **When Jesus rebuked someone or something, it didn't necessarily involve demonic forces.** The word *rebuke* appears twenty-seven times in the Gospels but only two other times in the rest of the New Testament. The Gospels tell us Jesus rebuked people (Matthew 16:22), demons (Luke 4:41), and infirmities (Luke 4:39), as well as the elements of nature like the wind (Mark 4:39). Although the act of rebuking takes on demonic overtones, it doesn't necessarily signify demonic activity. The Greek word *epitamao* means to charge someone as blamable, to admonish, or

reprove. The word wasn't directly associated with demons.

When Jesus rebuked a fever in Luke 4:39, we're given no indication that demonic forces made Simon's mother-in-law sick. In the same way, when Jesus rebuked the wind and the waves in Mark 4, the astonished disciples remarked, "Who is this? Even the wind and the waves obey him!" (Mark 4:41). The disciples were amazed that the wind and waves obeyed Jesus, not the demons.

4. **Demonic activity usually, but not always, involved non-physical afflictions.** The vast majority of times that the Gospels mention demonic involvement, the demons harass their victims without making them sick. For example, the Gerasene demoniac (how would you like that label pasted on you?) ran around the country naked, but he didn't suffer from any disease or malady (Mark 5). More often than not, demonic activity in the Gospels occurs in people whose malady might or might not be medically cured. The young boy suffering from seizures, in Luke 9, or the mute man, in Luke 11, appear to have suffered from spiritual disorders that carried physical manifestations. In other words, the cause (as opposed to the symptoms) couldn't be easily detected like being blind or lame. On the other hand, we do find the example of the lame woman Jesus healed, who had been "crippled by a spirit for eighteen years" (Luke 13:10–16).

5. **Deliverance was often set apart from physical healing.** When the Gospel writers described Jesus' ministry, they generally separated physical healing from deliverance. Mark comments, "And Jesus healed many who had various diseases. He also drove out many demons" (Mark 1:34). In the same way, Mark writes, "[The twelve disciples] drove out many demons and anointed many sick people with oil and healed them" (Mark 6:13). If deliverance and healing were one and the same, the sentence would read, "The disciples drove

out many demons, anointing many sick people with oil and healing them."

(If your eyes have glazed over from too many details, you can start reading again here!)

What does this tell us? Sometimes physical afflictions involve demonic activity and sometimes they don't. For those of us who crave formulas, it really messes things up. This forces us to pray and listen to the Holy Spirit. It also means we can't assume every sickness is an attack from the Enemy.

Making demonic activity our default setting is often an easy, perhaps lazy, approach to praying for healing. The majority of times, if you follow the pattern of Jesus' healing ministry, either Satan isn't involved at all or he plays a minor role behind the scenes.

So is all sickness a result of demonic activity? No. If you want to blame someone or something, blame Adam and Eve. All sickness, deterioration, and death result from their sin in the garden. Because we live in a fallen world, sickness will never be completely overcome until Jesus returns.

Should God Always Heal When We Pray?

Many charismatics believe that only one thing can stand between us and our healing: a lack of faith. Jesus only healed a few people in his hometown, because his family and friends didn't believe he could do it (Mark 6:4–6).

Critics claim that if the gift of healing was still in operation, people with the gift would be emptying the hospitals, healing everyone. But that's nonsense. Jesus didn't heal every sick person he encountered. He only healed those people in whom his Father was already at work (John 5:19).

When Jesus healed the invalid at the pool of Bethesda, he walked right through a crowd of blind, lame, and paralyzed people

(John 5:3). We know Jesus didn't hang around afterward to share the love because we read that "Jesus had slipped away into the crowd that was there" (John 5:13). Although both were within his power and privilege, Jesus didn't deliver his cousin John the Baptist from being beheaded, nor did he deliver himself from the cross.

The apostle Paul, undoubtedly second to Jesus in significance to the church, affirmed God's ability to heal, but even he didn't assume that everyone should be healed. Many scholars believe he suffered from an eye ailment. In an "obvious" sign of a lack of faith, Paul admitted not only that he suffered from an illness, but that he shared about his infirmity with the church in Galatia.

> Even though my illness was a trial to you, you did not treat me with contempt or scorn. Instead, you welcomed me as if I were an angel of God, as if I were Christ Jesus himself . . . I can testify that, if you could have done so, you would have torn out your eyes and given them to me.
>
> GALATIANS 4:14–15

Paul also advised Timothy to stop drinking water and imbibe a little wine for his stomach problems and other "frequent illnesses" (1 Timothy 5:23). And this isn't grape juice we're talking about here, it's the real thing. Paul must have been a true Episcopalian at heart!

The potholes we step into when praying for others lay in words like *all* and *everyone* and *always*. When we impose those expectations on God, we place him in our self-generated constraints.

Think about it: Insisting that God must act in a certain way actually makes him smaller rather than bigger. We define God according to our experiences, opinions, and limited earthly perspective. Obviously, God won't contradict his character or his Word, but we must be mindful of who is calling the shots.

I once heard John Wimber explain, "I don't know why God heals sometimes and other times he doesn't. All I know is that people get healed more often when you pray for them than when you don't."

God still heals just like he did in Bible times. We, on the other hand, can't heal. All we can do is pray for people and leave the results to God.

Throughout my life, I've prayed for people for healing. At times I've felt nothing, and the person was healed. Other times, I've sensed the Holy Spirit's presence and prayed what I call the "prayer of faith," and yet the person wasn't healed. How can we explain God?

> Have you ever come on anything quite like this extravagant generosity of God, this deep, deep wisdom? It's way over our heads. We'll never figure it out. Is there anyone around who can explain God? Anyone smart enough to tell him what to do? Anyone who has done him such a huge favor that God has to ask his advice? Everything comes from him; Everything happens through him; Everything ends up in him. Always glory! Always praise! Yes. Yes. Yes.
>
> ROMANS 11:33–36 (THE MESSAGE)

Okay, So Explain This!

In an odd, morbid irony, throughout the years many prominent healing evangelists and teachers have died from "abnormal" infirmities (especially cancer), rather than old age. Some hid their infirmities, possibly to avoid accusation of not being able to practice what they preach. But should this undermine our belief in God's ability to heal? Is this a sign of a curse from God? Absolutely not!

Perhaps God allowed these men and women to die in this manner to remind us that he is God and we are not. He is the one who not only heals, but decides who will be healed—regardless of our opinions or perspectives.

Harking back to the previous chapter, if God is truly sovereign, then we can't say he must heal every time, according to our time-table.

When that revelation hit me, my world turned upside-down. *I'm not God nor do I have the right to dictate his actions to him—nor does he owe me any explanation.*

While detoxing from my past conception of healing, I found myself wrestling with doubt and cynicism toward anything associated with it. At times I even doubted God's willingness to heal at all.

How can we know when it's God's will to heal and when it isn't? We don't. All I know is that we live in a fallen world. And at times God sovereignly chooses to shoot a beam of eternity into our mortal existence.

So if God doesn't always heal, what good can come out of it? I'm glad you asked!

CHAPTER 16

You Know It Hurts So Good (No, Really!)

The Role of Pain and Suffering in Our Charismatic Beliefs

Sitting on my bookshelf is a copy of *The Holiest of All*—a reader-friendly exposition on the book of Hebrews written by Andrew Murray. The book is a classic, evidenced by the fact that it has been in print since 1894.

The particular copy I own was distributed by a television ministry from the Word of Faith camp. Rarely do television preachers promote books written by non-charismatics, especially those that existed before Agnes Ozman (as I explained in chapter 4).

Since the book of Hebrews addresses the subject of suffering, I was curious as to why the ministry was giving the book away. But when I looked closer at my copy, I realized it was an abridged edition. In the foreword, the television preacher writes:

> As we prepared this abridged edition of *The Holiest of All*, I requested to delete three chapters and one paragraph from the original text, because they centered on suffering being the will

of God. . . . Even today many are still held captive to this belief. One of the most effective strategies of Satan within the church is to convince people that God causes bad things to come into their lives.

Is pain and suffering bad? Does God cause bad things to happen to us?

Empty—or at Least Partial—Promises

Every spring Christian bookstores stock their shelves with Bible promise books that make great gifts for high school and college graduates. I'm not sure any graduate reads them, but at a minimum, it alleviates the consciences of caring relatives concerned that their niece or nephew keep the faith.

In my earlier years, I assembled quite a collection of these books, many with leather-bound covers and my name engraved in gold on the front. Page after page of Scriptures promising the perfect life made me feel all warm and fuzzy inside. *How can I ever fail?* I thought.

All of us subconsciously pursue the perfect life. A family. Kids. Provision. Health. The abundant life. Word of Faith teachers tell us that we can—and should—have the perfect life here on earth. We just need to stand on the promises of God's Word.

But as helpful and inspiring as these Bible promise books are, one promise is conspicuously absent from all of them, straight from the lips of Jesus: "In the world you will have tribulation" (John 16:33 ESV). That's a promise from Jesus you can take to the bank—although I refused to believe it in my earlier years.

Perhaps our desire for the "perfect life" needs to be re-examined.

Friedrich Nietzsche, the nineteenth-century philosopher, proposed a way of living in many ways similar to the perfect life prescribed in the Bible promise books. The son and grandson of

Lutheran ministers, Nietzsche suggested that man was stepping into the era of the *Superman*, the self-determined individual who trusts in himself and needs no one else. A man who continuously improves himself, overcoming his problems.

Superman's goal? To become better, stronger, faster, smarter, self-sufficient. To extract all the enjoyment he can from this life. Superman doesn't need anyone else nor does he need God, because he lives as a god unto himself (sound familiar?). Superman feels no pain; he overcomes suffering by a sheer act of the will.

In many ways, our pursuits are no different than Nietzsche's. We try to make ourselves impervious to pain. Sticks and stones may break my bones but words will never hurt me. We avoid pain and suffering at all costs. Years ago the chorus of a popular song began with the words, "Don't cry out loud. Just keep it inside you." Like Superman in our comic books and cartoons on television, we try to make bullets bounce off our chest.

No Pain, No Gain

Jesus, however, chose a much different way than Michael J. Klassen or Friedrich Nietzsche's Superman. The author of Hebrews describes Jesus this way: "In bringing many sons to glory, it was fitting that God, for whom and through whom everything exists, should make the author of their salvation perfect through suffering" (Hebrews 2:10).

Did you read the last part of that verse? *God made Jesus perfect through suffering.* That doesn't mean Jesus was imperfect before he was nailed to the cross. The Greek word for perfect, *teleio-o*, means "complete," or "to carry out your purpose." Think about it: Jesus carried out his God-ordained purpose by suffering and dying on the cross in our place.

The author of Hebrews continues,

Since the children have flesh and blood, he too shared in their humanity so that by his death he might destroy him who holds

the power of death—that is, the devil—and free those who all
their lives were held in slavery by their fear of death.

HEBREWS 2:14–15

Jesus, the Son of God and Creator of the world, willingly
divested himself of the privileges of heaven to suffer on our behalf.
And through his death, he destroyed the power of death and freed
those who were enslaved by the fear of death. Jesus wasn't afraid
of pain and suffering because he knew they couldn't kill him.

When you belong to Jesus, pain cannot kill you. That doesn't mean
you won't die a physical death. Jesus said, "Do not be afraid of those
who kill the body but cannot kill the soul" (Matthew 10:28).

The author here is addressing two fundamental fears, the fear
of pain and the fear of death. His message is this: To the Christian,
death doesn't exist. So why are we afraid of pain? When we belong to
Jesus, pain and suffering cannot kill us. So what if we die? What's the
worst thing that can happen to us? We get our reward, something far
better than the "perfect life" this world has to offer—eternal life and
an unhindered relationship with the Father, Son, and Holy Spirit!

A little further on, the author of Hebrews writes,

So, as the Holy Spirit says: "Today, if you hear his voice, do not
harden your hearts as you did in the rebellion, during the time
of testing in the desert, where your fathers tested and tried me
and for forty years saw what I did."

HEBREWS 3:7–9

All of us face two alternatives in dealing with our pain. The
first alternative is to harden our hearts. The passage above says,
"Do not harden your hearts as you did in the rebellion, during the
time of testing in the desert. . . ."

This passage is a quote from Psalm 95, but it tells the story of
the children of Israel in Exodus 17. The Israelites were wander-
ing in the desert before entering the Promised Land when they

ran out of water. We can only go a few days without water before we die.

The Israelites were suffering—they were dying of thirst—and they started to complain. They asked God why he brought them into the desert and they begged him to take them back to Egypt. In fact, they got so worked up that they were ready to stone Moses. I can't say that I blame the Israelites for their reaction.

So God told Moses to strike the rock at Mount Horeb. Moses struck the rock and water came out. God then named the place *Massah* and *Meribah*, which mean "testing" and "quarreling."

In the midst of their trouble, the people hardened their hearts toward God. Like many of us when we face pain and suffering, they questioned God's goodness, his faithfulness, and his willingness to act on their behalf.

This was Adam and Eve's faulty assumption in the garden: God isn't good; God cannot be trusted; God isn't enough. In many ways, the Israelites wanted to become Nietzsche's Superman—self-sufficient people who didn't need God, who yearned for lives devoid of trouble. Most ironic of all, they yearned to return to their former lives of slavery. As a result, the Israelites wandered in the wilderness for forty years.

Although Friedrich Nietzsche aspired to become Superman, he couldn't live up to his own beliefs. As he grew older, he became increasingly irrational and ended up in an insane asylum. He spent the last twelve years of his life under the care of his mother—a woman who loved Jesus.

When we experience pain, suffering, and loss, the overwhelming temptation is to harden our hearts. We can harden our hearts in a variety of ways.

- Blaming God

- Blaming Satan

- Blaming the people who cause the suffering

- Numbing the pain (through food, fantasy, disengagement, anger, addictions, etc.)

- Denying the pain

Our tendency is to go anywhere but feel the pain.

I don't want to minimize anyone's pain. Pain hurts. Suffering can feel unbearable. But we no longer need to be enslaved by the fear of death! Pain isn't the enemy! It can kill the body, but pain cannot—cannot!—kill the soul.

When we try to bounce bullets off our chest by denying the pain or immediately rebuking it, we end up hardening our hearts. Toward God and toward others. You see, there are perils with playing Superman.

The Perils of Playing Superman

George Reeves was an aspiring actor in the 1930s and '40s. He holds the distinction of speaking the opening lines in the movie *Gone With the Wind*. Prognosticators predicted greatness for George Reeves, but just as his career started taking off, he was called into military service and served in World War II. When he returned from the war, his prospects had all dried up and he was left to play bit parts in "B" movies.

In 1951, George Reeves reluctantly accepted the offer to play Superman in the new television series. Especially in those days, television was considered the bottom of the food chain in the entertainment industry, but Reeves had no other options.

Almost overnight, George Reeves became Superman in American culture. And by the time the series concluded in 1957, Reeves was so firmly entrenched as America's Superman that he could find no other acting roles.

The pain of a disappointing acting career drove him to harden his heart. And to anesthetize the pain, he became a heavy drinker.

Think about the irony: The man of steel, who could make bullets bounce off his chest, couldn't handle real pain. Rather than feel it, he chose to numb himself from it.

Two years later, after a night of drinking with his friends, Superman walked up the stairs in his home to lie down. Moments later, gunshots rang out from his room. The man of steel lay sprawled out on his bed, with a gunshot wound to his head.

An air of mystery surrounds George Reeves' death because there are some indications that he may have been murdered. But nonetheless, Superman died an unhappy man who couldn't face the overwhelming burden of his own pain.

The man of steel, impervious to pain, died of a hardening of the heart.

The fundamental response to pain and suffering is self-protection. We think that by hardening our hearts—by ignoring or rebuking the pain—we save ourselves from it. But in the process, our attempts at self-preservation only deaden it.

The Other Response to Pain

When we face pain, suffering, and disappointment, we really have only two alternatives—to become like Superman and harden our hearts or bring our brokenness to Jesus.

In the midst of his discussion on pain and suffering, the author of Hebrews offers these words: "Therefore, holy brothers, who share in the heavenly calling, fix your thoughts on Jesus, the apostle and high priest whom we confess" (Hebrews 3:1).

In the midst of pain and suffering, the author doesn't say:

- "Curse the suffering" or
- "Bind and rebuke the spirits of suffering" or
- "Ignore the pain" or
- "Exercise the faith to overcome it."

He says, "Fix your thoughts on Jesus."

The Greek word for *fix* means to consider, notice, but more so to direct your whole mind to an object, to immerse yourself in it. To fix your thoughts on Jesus means to lose yourself in Christ. When we fix our thoughts on Jesus we ask ourselves:

- How did Jesus suffer?
- How have *I* inflicted the same kind of suffering on Christ?
- How does Jesus respond to suffering?
- What was his attitude toward it?
- Where is he present in my suffering and how can I know him more through it?

Through questions like these we can truly understand the meaning of Philippians 3:10: "I want to know Christ and the power of his resurrection and *the fellowship of sharing in his sufferings*" (italics added).

Feeling our pain doesn't mean we share it only with Jesus. For this reason the author of Hebrews writes, "But encourage one another daily, as long as it is called Today, so that none of you may be hardened by sin's deceitfulness" (Hebrews 3:13).

Rather than ignore the pain, we acknowledge it. Rather than keep the pain to ourselves, we explore it with others. Rather than let it fester in the darkness, we bring it into the light. We share our pain with each other and gain strength from the sharing of it.

And what happens? The weight of a hardened heart is lifted.

Perfect Suffering

Later in the book of Hebrews, we read about the types of suffering that the great men and women of faith endured, and then we read these astonishing words: "God had planned something better for us so that only together with us would they be made perfect" (Hebrews 11:40).

There's that word perfect again. Complete. *Teleio-o*. The same word used to describe Jesus. Jesus carried out his purpose through suffering. In the same way, these great men and women of faith carried out their purpose through suffering.

Like us, Jesus didn't want to experience the pain of the cross. He begged God to remove the cup of suffering, then he uttered words that continually hound me: "Yet not my will, but yours be done" (Luke 22:42). What was God's will for Jesus? That he endure the cross.

In the same way, charismatics fully understand the power of the Holy Spirit resident within them. We know firsthand the power of the name of Jesus to withstand the wiles of the Enemy. Like Jesus, we all want to avoid the cup of suffering.

Perhaps there is a redemptive element to our suffering. Perhaps our pain isn't in vain. Perhaps there's more to this life than this life.

One of my most formative experiences surrounded a tremendously painful church situation. Some people treated me quite unfairly, with the intent to hurt me. I, on the other hand, didn't always respond like I should have. Years later, as I look back, I'd have to say I don't regret the experience—although I'd never want to repeat it. I'm different, and hopefully better, as a result of it.

So is pain and suffering bad? Paul didn't seem to think so. He invited Timothy, his protégé, to "join [him] in suffering for the gospel, by the power of God" (2 Timothy 1:8).

I guess it really depends on how you define the word *bad*. From our perspective—and especially in the moment—pain and suffering always seem bad. But looking at them in retrospect, we often find that God can use them in very redemptive ways.

To quote C. S. Lewis, "God whispers to us in our pleasures, speaks in our conscience, but shouts in our pains: it is His megaphone to rouse a deaf world." I wish God spoke to my heart as clearly in the good times as he does in the bad. Perhaps the problem isn't in the volume of his voice as it is in my willingness to listen. Pain brings me to the end of myself. It helps me realize that I don't have this life figured out.

Lewis further explains, "[Pain] removes the veil; it plants the flag of truth within the fortress of a rebel soul." The rebel soul. Sounds reminiscent of the hardened heart described in the book of Hebrews.

Is sickness, pain, and death the worst thing that can happen to a person? Although I wouldn't wish it on anyone, if I can remove myself from the suffering, I'd have to answer no. A hardened heart toward God is the worst thing.

God may deliver us from our sickness and pain, but if our hearts are hard, we're just as far away from him after we're healed as we were before. Sickness and pain, however, help us realize our bankruptcy without Jesus and drive us to him.

So what do we do with all those passages in Scripture that promise the life of our dreams? We can't ignore them. Quite often—more often than we realize, I think—God blesses us with good things (and I could sure use another generous helping of those!). But we can't define God according to our desires. Books in the Bible promising blessing for the righteous are countered by books like Ecclesiastes and events such as the crucifixion and the martyrdom of the saints in Acts.

At times our pain and suffering result from a direct demonic attack. Every lingering illness in my family is treated as such. But every time I try to stuff God into a prefabricated box, he finds a way of getting out. At times, by resisting our suffering, we may in fact find ourselves resisting God.

So what is our hope in the midst of the pain? Let's go back to the promise Jesus gave us: "In the world you will have tribulation. *But take heart; I have overcome the world*" (John 16:33 ESV, italics added). Jesus has overcome the world. If you can trust him with eternal life, you can trust him with your life, as well.

With this in mind, let's look at what the life of faith looks like.

CHAPTER 17

Blood, Sweat, and Tears . . . Or Not

The Definition of True Faith

"I conducted a funeral for a woman from our church yesterday," the well-known charismatic megachurch pastor reported to his congregation one Sunday morning. "I told the people attending the funeral how much we loved this woman and hated to see her suffer from cancer like she did. It was a tragedy that she died, because she didn't have to. She didn't need to.

"So you know what I had to do at the funeral?" he continued. "I apologized and told them, 'I'm sorry your loved one had to die. It was our fault, because if we would have had enough faith, she wouldn't have died.' "

Then looking at his congregation, the pastor repeated himself, "It's our fault that our beloved sister died, because we didn't have enough faith!"

Ouch!

Although I don't condone abusive behavior like this, I can understand the pastor's reason for admonishing his congregation. This story is true, by the way.

Perhaps the Word of Faith People Were on to Something

Whether or not you agree with the Word of Faith teachers, they understand the importance of living by faith. Scripture tells us, "Without faith it is impossible to please God" (Hebrews 11:6). *Impossible* is a pretty strong word. The passage doesn't say without faith it is difficult or challenging to please God. It uses one of those extreme words that usually shows up when we're either really excited or really sad (or really mad!).

Paul follows this same line of thinking by writing, "Everything that does not come from faith is sin" (Romans 14:23). There's one of those extreme words again: *everything*. He furthermore explains, "The only thing that counts is faith expressing itself through love" (Galatians 5:6). Apparently God values faith and rejects anything that doesn't come from faith.

So what is faith, how do we get it, and what does it look like?

Due to abuse and overuse, *faith* has evolved into an ambiguous word that means different things to different people—with different Christian camps establishing their own definitions.

Christian mainliners (people from historic Christian denominations that began before Agnes Ozman—except our Southern Baptist friends) usually define faith as a "*belief* system," like Hinduism, Islam, or Christianity. They might use the word like this: "Jared has a strong faith, which explains why he keeps talking with his friends about Jesus." Or they may use the word as a means of encouraging people to persevere when they're discouraged, like, "Hey, John—keep the faith!"

Evangelical non-charismatics (independent Bible churches and most denominations that started after dear old Agnes, bless her heart!) begin with the same definition, but strongly *believe* in the Bible's authority and authenticity. Their faith resides in the certainty that the Bible is historically true. The children of Israel passed through the Red Sea on dry land. Jesus walked on the water (not a sandbar), miraculously fed the five thousand, and rose from the dead. Evangelical non-charismatics also proclaim the importance of placing our faith, or *trust*, in Jesus as our personal Lord and Savior in order to receive eternal life. Some refer to this as "saving faith." (Incidentally, fundamentalists fit into this definition, as well.)

Charismatics are evangelicals on steroids. They believe what happened in the Bible is true—and have the faith to believe that it can happen today, as well. Jesus walked on the water . . . and so can you! Jesus healed . . . and so can you! Jesus fed the five thousand . . . and so can you! You could even raise the dead if you spent that morning in the Word, found the right verse to confess, and yelled loud enough over the dead body. Okay, okay, I'm overstating myself, but that's the general idea. Charismatics believe that because the Holy Spirit lives in us, we're more than conquerors. To the charismatic, faith is *something you do*, not merely something you believe.

These definitions are overgeneralizations, of course, but you get the point.

Which camp is correct? All three. Charismatics just tend to gravitate to the extreme definitions in their Bible dictionary.

The word *faith* appears in a few scattered places in the Old Testament but plays a very prominent role in the New Testament. Variations of the word appear over five hundred times between Matthew and Revelation. Paul ranked it in importance with hope and love, with the greatest being love (1 Corinthians 13:13).

If you were to give it an overarching definition, you could say that faith means to believe or trust. If you believe or trust that Jesus died on the cross and removed from you the penalty of sin, then you will be saved. The system of doctrine surrounding this truth is called our belief system. When charismatics exercise their faith when praying for someone, they are trusting God to intervene on their behalf.

Is Faith Just Another Word for Sweat?

Years ago I watched a cheesy vampire movie that became for me, at the time, a spiritual experience. At a critical juncture in the movie, the vampire killer confronts the vampire.

Holding a cross in front of him, the vampire killer yells, "Back, spawn of Satan!"

"Oh, really?" the vampire replies. "You have to have faith for this to work on me!" Then he grabs the cross, crushes it, and throws it aside. If you're a little rusty on your vampire trivia, crosses reportedly render vampires powerless.

Later in the movie, the vampire killer again confronts the vampire. This time, however, he looks intently at the cross and wills within himself the faith to believe in its power. The vampire killer then vanquishes his nemesis.

Like the vampire killer, I envisioned myself willing the faith to overcome any obstacle. Faith was equivalent to sweat—I just needed to push it out (without giving myself an aneurysm!).

In my charismatic experience, faith was the result of blood, sweat, and tears. The longer I prayed, the louder I shouted, the more Scriptures I quoted, the more I whipped myself into a frenzy, the greater the measure of faith that would materialize.

Does faith come from blood, sweat, and tears? Although I may exercise the faith to move mountains, faith nevertheless begins with God.

The author of Hebrews describes Jesus as "the author and perfecter of our faith" (Hebrews 12:2). The Greek word for author means "originator" or "initiator." Jesus gave to us the faith—the good news of the Gospel—which we believe. Without his initiative, we would have no faith to believe in, and no faith to believe *with*.

Paul writes that "by grace you have been saved, through faith . . . it is the gift of God" (Ephesians 2:8). The faith we express in believing and receiving Christ comes from God, not us. If we can amass the faith within ourselves to believe in Jesus, then salvation is no longer a gift. Furthermore, Paul exhorted his readers to evaluate themselves with sober judgment, "in accordance with the measure of faith God has given [them]" (Romans 12:3).

We cannot generate within ourselves the faith we need to please God. We cannot have faith in our faith, because faith doesn't come from us. If it did, we wouldn't need God, and we would all be "little gods."

So we're stuck! Without faith we cannot please God; everything that doesn't come from faith is sin. Yet we cannot generate our own faith.

So how do we get it?

Paul wrote, "Faith comes by hearing, and hearing by the word of God" (Romans 10:17 NKJV). The Word preached in church builds our faith. In Paul's day, Christians didn't own a selection of different scrolls they could read in the morning before leaving for work. In fact, in the very early days of the church, not even written fragments of the New Testament existed. The only New Testament material the congregations had at their disposal were oral traditions of Jesus' words and works, which later became the basis of the Gospels. In this passage, Paul was referring to hearing the Old Testament read and preached when the believers gathered on Sundays.

Today we can listen to the Word of God preached, but we can also read it for ourselves. So faith comes by reading the Word of God, as well. Again, I must give the Word of Faith teachers credit here. They know the power of the Word of God to embolden us with faith.

The measure of faith every believer receives—even as small as a mustard seed—comes from God. Hearing, reading, and meditating on it waters those seeds. In the same way, as we listen and commune with Jesus, the Word made flesh, our faith is built up.

And at times God supernaturally gives us a measure of faith to believe that he can, and will, intervene.

Saints of Whom the World Was Not Worthy

So we know what faith is and where it comes from. But I'd like to offer you another snapshot of faith that might not have surfaced in your charismatic experience.

Ask a charismatic to point you to a man or woman of faith, and who do you think they would point you to?

Benny Hinn or Oral Roberts.

Your pastor at church who publicly depended upon God to supply the money to finance the next building project—and God supplied the need.

A family friend who refused to accept the ravages of cancer and overcame it, coming through with a clean bill of health.

All of these are great examples. In our charismatic faith, we often point to the overcomers as models of faith.

But something has stuck in my craw about how we define faith. When Paul explains the armor of God—a favorite passage of Scripture among our charismatic kin—he describes the battle this way:

> Therefore put on the full armor of God, so that when the day of evil comes, you may be able to stand your ground, and after you have done everything, to stand.
>
> EPHESIANS 6:13

What's the picture of the valiant warrior in this passage? Standing. Just . . . standing. Not overcoming. Not stomping on the Enemy's head. Just surviving. If you've been beat up in a tough battle, this should come as a relief. You don't always have to emerge from a struggle with the victory in hand. Sometimes, oftentimes, all you can do is survive. That's good news.

Faith can mean obtaining a promise from God and holding on to that promise until it's fulfilled. However, the author of Hebrews paints a much different picture of faith.

Many Christians identify Hebrews 11 as faith's Hall of Fame. It begins with the definition of faith—"the substance of things hoped for, the evidence of things not seen" (Hebrews 11:1 KJV). Then it lists examples of faith in action beginning with God and concluding with David, Samuel, and the prophets.

According to the chapter, the great heroes of faith conquer kingdoms, rout armies, and receive back their dead. We all want to be heroes like them!

But then the end of the chapter gives us a completely different picture of the life of faith: torture, jeers, floggings, imprisonment, being sawed in two, destitution, persecution, mistreatment. They wander in deserts and mountains, and live in caves and holes in the ground. "The world was not worthy of them," the writer reflects on the men and women who drank from the common cup of suffering (Hebrews 11:38).

Wait a minute! This doesn't fit into our definition of faith. Those poor souls must have uttered a negative confession or suffered from a generational curse.

I'm not sure I want that kind of faith. Isn't there a different kind of faith God desires, the kind that gives us our best life *now*?

Then the writer concludes with a profound comment that brings perspective to my chaotic, self-absorbed life: "And all these, though commended through their faith, did not receive what was promised" (Hebrews 11:39 ESV).

What is the picture of faith? It isn't the fulfillment of the promise before we die; it's dying with the promise unfulfilled. It's holding on to the promise in the face of overwhelming circumstances that whisper, "Give up!" It's "keeping the faith," according to the mainline Christians as defined a few pages back.

Some people would see this as discouraging, but I find it

tremendously encouraging. Just because God doesn't answer all my prayers doesn't mean I'm a failure at living by faith. Perhaps holding on to Jesus in the middle of a past church firestorm—which I partially brought upon myself—was a greater exercise of faith than when I prayed for a person who was healed.

It All Depends on Where You Call "Home"

Earlier the author of Hebrews explains,

> All these people were still living by faith when they died. They did not receive the things promised; they only saw them and welcomed them from a distance. And they admitted that they were aliens and strangers on earth.
>
> HEBREWS 11:13

According to this passage, men and women of faith consider themselves "aliens" and "strangers." In Bible times, aliens were the poorest people in their society. So poor, in fact, that God commanded the farmers to harvest their fields only once so the widows and aliens could glean the leftovers (Leviticus 23:22). The word *stranger* could also be translated "transient." Aliens and transients hold their possessions loosely and admit that their home isn't really their home.

And where is home?

Heaven. "Instead, they were longing for a better country—a heavenly one. Therefore God is not ashamed to be called their God, for he has prepared a city for them" (Hebrews 11:16). We long for heaven, but even deeper, we long for heaven on earth—the new earth, which will someday be our home for eternity (you can read about it in Revelation 21-22).

Men and women of faith recognize that this world is not our home; our home is heaven. Sometimes we receive a partial reward in this life, but always in the life to come. Knowing that the reward of our faith will come to complete fruition in the next life forces us to look deeply into our motivation. Are we focusing our desires on a world that will too quickly pass away, or the new earth that will last for eternity? Does our faith rest on immediate gratification, or on the eternal promise? If it rests on immediate gratification, we lose faith when God doesn't come through within the parameters of our timeline.

God called Abraham to leave family and friends to move to an unknown land where he would live as a transient in a tent. God promised to give the land to his descendants. Yet when Abraham died, the promise was still unfulfilled. Nevertheless, Abraham believed God. Six hundred years later, the children of Israel began occupying it! Talk about a visionary and a great man of faith! But in the end, he understood that the Promised Land served as a portent—a pointer—to the true land of promise that God has prepared for each one of us.

Perhaps like Abraham, God gave you a promise that has still gone unfulfilled. Maybe the promise involved provision or the salvation of your family. If God's promise to you still remains unanswered, don't give up and don't beat yourself up. Do everything within your control, then stand. God is good, he knows what he is doing, and he's in control.

If you've been beat up by other charismatics for not having enough faith, first of all, consider the possibility that their intentions were partially good. They wanted you to live by faith so you could please God. But perhaps their definition of faith was really nothing more than blood, sweat, and tears. Their futile efforts of trying to force faith out of you probably did more damage than good. But a previous negative experience with faith makes a weak excuse for living a faithless life.

In my faith journey as a charismatic, I'm continually forced to let go of my negative experiences and allow God to redefine what faith looks like to me. I need to pursue a life of faith, leaving the results to God and remembering that my true home lies in heaven.

Before concluding our discussion on faith, we probably ought to examine the role of feelings—because we all know feelings play a pretty big role in the life of a charismatic. Let's take a look. . . .

CHAPTER 18

More Than a Feeling

Is It Okay to Pursue a Spiritual Buzz?

In a church where I used to serve as an assistant pastor, a lovely soft-spoken woman attended whom God had called into the healing ministry. An older woman, she was a carryover from the days of Kathryn Kuhlman, the great healing evangelist.

This dear lady spoke in various churches around the area, and once or twice a year held a healing service at our church on a Sunday night. Attending one of her services was both satisfying and strange.

As one particular meeting began, our little church building was only half filled, which meant about seventy-five people were sitting in the pews. After the singing concluded, she preached a forty-five minute sermon. It was a pretty basic sermon on healing. She wasn't an overly dynamic speaker, but nevertheless she gave a solid message.

Toward the end of her talk, I looked over my shoulder and noticed that the sanctuary was beginning to fill with people. Rather than take their seats, they stood in a long line along the back wall, as if they were waiting for her sermon to conclude.

Every pastor sees people leaving before the end of the sermon. People never show up at the end of the sermon—except in the spring, on the weekend Daylight Saving Time begins. In those cases, we want to point to the embarrassed soul and yell, "Hey everyone, look at the goof who forgot to change his clock last night!" Anyway, the preacher knows when people leave before the end of the sermon, because we can see them as they walk out the doors. But in some freakish reversal in the polarities of the time-space continuum, during this particular church service, people were showing up toward the end.

At the conclusion of the sermon, I understood the purpose of this strange phenomenon. Apparently everywhere the woman ministered, she formed a healing line at the front. Many of the people standing in the back were just moments away from being slain in the Spirit.

If you're a charismatic newbie, being "slain in the Spirit" happens when someone prays for you and the Holy Spirit falls on you in such a powerful way that you lose control and fall backward onto the floor, worshiping Jesus. Fortunately, the woman used specially trained "catchers" who caught the men and women before they hit the ground.

Her groupies knew the routine. Rather than bother with listening to the message, they knew about how far into the service she would begin praying for people. Hence the crowd at the back.

As the woman formed the healing line, waves of men and women began flooding into the back of the building. What began with seventy-five people quickly multiplied to probably two hundred. The experience was surreal. Toward the end of the evening, fifteen or twenty people were lying on the floor, slain in the Spirit.

Then a man came running in, breathing heavily, looking around for the healing evangelist. When he spotted her, he walked straight up to her, she prayed for him, and he immediately fell to the floor. About five minutes later he stood up and walked out of the church. Total time spent at church that night: not more than eight minutes.

What astonished me about the evening was the importance these people placed on getting their spiritual buzz.

What role do feelings play in our faith? Do we need a spiritual buzz to make sure we're okay? Does the occurrence of a spiritual buzz assure me that everything is good between me and God?

Believe It or Not, Spiritual Buzzes Are Biblical . . .

Walter Hollenweger, a noted scholar on Pentecostal and charismatic studies, once commented, "Pentecostals and [Christian] Liberals are twins. Liberals base everything on experience but haven't any; Pentecostals base everything on experience and they have it."[1]

What separates Pentecostals and charismatics from many of our non-charismatic counterparts is that we not only claim to do "the stuff," but we get to experience "the stuff," as well. Reminiscent of a "don't muzzle the ox" kind of thing. We believe that God interacts with humanity in tangible, life-changing ways. And no one can take away our experience.

My life was changed at winter camp in the seventh grade when our camp speaker prophesied that I would someday become a pastor. While he spoke over me, I felt an energy surging through my body like nothing I'd experienced before. For forty-five minutes the presence of the Holy Spirit froze me in my chair.

Afterward, no one had to convince me that God was real or that I would someday become a pastor.

Critics of Pentecostals and charismatics claim that our faith is built on experience. But if you look at Scripture, it becomes apparent very quickly that experiential encounters with God played a significant role in the faith of our spiritual predecessors:

- God appeared to Abraham in the form of three men (like the Trinity), promising that someday he and Sarah would have a son of their own.

- Jacob wrestled all night with an angel of the Lord.

- Joshua spoke with the same angel—likely the preincarnate Christ—before conquering Jericho.

- God spoke to Moses from a burning bush.

- Gabriel appeared to Mary, the mother of Jesus, in a dream.

- Tongues of fire appeared on the heads of the first Christians at Pentecost.

- And of course, we have the many miracles Jesus performed.

Despite the countless miracle stories in Scripture, what speaks to me most clearly are the words of John the apostle:

> That which was from the beginning, which we have heard, which we have seen with our eyes, which we have looked at and our hands have touched—this we proclaim concerning the Word of life. The life appeared; we have seen it and testify to it, and we proclaim to you the eternal life, which was with the Father and has appeared to us. We proclaim to you what we have seen and heard, so that you also may have fellowship with us. And our fellowship is with the Father and with his Son, Jesus Christ.
>
> 1 JOHN 1:1–3

What would motivate John to concoct a fictional story about Jesus? He risked his life for the gospel because he had heard and seen and touched the Word made flesh. His experience with Jesus forever changed him. In the same vein, Peter wrote, "We did not follow cleverly invented stories when we told you about the power and coming of our Lord Jesus Christ, but we were eyewitnesses of his majesty" (2 Peter 1:16).

In tandem, Peter and John remarked, "We cannot help speaking about what we have seen and heard" (Acts 4:20). They didn't say, "We cannot help speaking about what Scripture says." They testified to their experience.

It seems to me that the astonishing growth of the charismatic movement is most attributed to the palpable experience charismatics have with God. Experiences with God play a significant role in our life of faith. A spiritual life devoid of experience can appear devoid of life.

Now, before you start throwing stones at me, please understand that I'm not trying to criticize the faith of many sincere Christians who have never experienced a touch of the divine. But until the twentieth century, spiritual experiences were commonly accepted. In fact, part of the reason the Roman Catholic Church has received the charismatic renewal so readily is because they have historically and theologically made room for otherworldly experiences. The influence of modernist philosophy has minimized the acceptance of the existence of God, and of his interaction with us.

. . . But Remember That Strange Fire Can Look Like Holy Fire

The validity of spiritual experience does not imply that all spiritual experiences are created equal. Just because a dynamic speaker claims to work signs and wonders does not mean the signs and wonders come from God. Paul tells us that "Satan . . . masquerades as an angel of light" (2 Corinthians 11:14).

Jesus warned that false Christs and false prophets would perform great signs and miracles that deceive many (Matthew 24:24). Furthermore, Paul warned that in the last days, "The work of Satan [will be] displayed in all kinds of counterfeit miracles, signs and wonders" (2 Thessalonians 2:9).

In charismatic circles, we too often assume that if God uses someone in a mighty way, the person must be speaking and acting on behalf of God without error. How could God use someone with whom he wasn't pleased?

Regardless of the magnitude of the miracle, the vividness of the vision, or the specificity of the fulfilled prophecy, we cannot automatically assume the work or word came from God. In fact, the nature of strange fire and holy fire is that the two often appear at the same time. Whenever the Spirit appears, the flesh is surely one step behind. And sometimes the flesh jumps one step ahead of the Spirit.

Furthermore, the exercise of spiritual gifts has little to do with character. King Saul once broke into spontaneous prophecy, but that didn't mean everything was good between him and God (see 1 Samuel 10:10–11). "God's gifts and his call are irrevocable," we read in Romans 11:29. Regardless of what we do, our gifts and call from God remain the same.

Although God used A. A. Allen to impact the lives of many people through his healing and deliverance ministry in the 1950s and '60s, he also reportedly suffered from alcoholism. In the same way, Jim Bakker enjoyed a thriving television ministry at the same time he indulged in a tryst with his secretary, Jessica Hahn. Charles Parham, who presided over the prayer meeting when Agnes Ozman spoke in tongues, was a racist and exhibited strong leanings toward the Ku Klux Klan.

Just as our leaders can be used of God in spite of their faults, God can move mightily through us in spite of our faults. In fact, if he waited for us to get our act together before using us or moving within us, he'd still be waiting.

Regarding our experiences with God, we must be spiritually discerning and biblically literate. But we must also avoid the laziness that prompts people to immediately believe every word that proceeds from the mouth of their pastor or favorite television preacher—all of whom could be interpreting Scripture through a very fleshy, partial lens. The same applies to the words I'm writing in this book.

In other words, experiences are good—but we must run them through the grid of Scripture. And if we run them through the grid of Scripture—our bedrock foundation—then they cannot serve as the foundation of our walk with God.

When asked to prove he was the Messiah, Jesus remarked, "A wicked and adulterous generation asks for a miraculous sign!" (Matthew 12:39). His life and his words were sufficient for the people in his day to believe. In fact, when you consider all the miracles Jesus worked in his three-year ministry, it's astounding how many of his disciples were with him at the cross. Only one—John. An experience with God was not enough. Signs may *accompany* those who believe (Mark 16:17–18), but they cannot form the bedrock of our belief.

So what role *should* our spiritual experiences play in our walk with God?

We All Need to Raise Our Ebenezers

A weak, defenseless country can take plundering only so long. Their repeated looting at the hands of the Philistines rendered Israel discouraged and weak. Finally, after exhausting nearly all their options, they turned to God. Isn't that how it usually works?

Under the leadership of Samuel the prophet, the Israelites rid themselves of their many gods and committed themselves to serving the one true God. Then the nation gathered together in Mizpah, where they fasted, prayed, and confessed their sins. Knowing that mobilizing the people would likely result in an organized, unified defense, the Philistines rallied their forces to fight God's chosen people.

Despite their newfound enthusiasm and purpose, the people of Israel knew their army was far outmatched by their well-equipped enemies. Their only hope was in the God of Israel.

While Samuel offered a burnt sacrifice on behalf of the people, the Philistine garrisons stationed themselves nearby to engage them in battle. Suddenly thunder sounded from above, throwing the attacking army into a panic. The men of Israel left their prayer meeting and attacked the Philistines, routing them in surprising fashion.

Afterward Samuel set up a stone outside of Mizpah and named it Ebenezer, which means "stone of help" (1 Samuel 7:12).

Throughout Israel's Old Testament history, we read about these stones of remembrance. The morning after Jacob dreamed of choirs of angels ascending and descending a stairway to heaven and God's promise to bless him, he set up a stone of remembrance (Genesis 28). After God parted the Jordan River, allowing the children of Israel to enter the Promised Land, they gathered twelve stones from the riverbed and erected a memorial of stones commemorating God's faithfulness (Joshua 3).

Stones of remembrance serve as reminders of God's goodness, love, and faithfulness. On my desk sits a stand-up wooden carving of a map of Mozambique, which is adjacent to South Africa. Over the years, I've helped lead mission teams who shared Jesus with these dear, impoverished people. And as much as I've shared Jesus with them, they have probably shared more of the love of Jesus with me. Often when I look at the map, I think of the stories of God's faithfulness that I experienced while I was there. That wooden carving serves as a "stone of remembrance" of sorts.

In the same way, our special touches from the Holy Spirit serve as reminders of God's goodness, love, and faithfulness. Like the stones of remembrance, these altars are important but not essential. At times the Israelites worshiped at the altars of remembrance. In the same way, we can easily worship our experience of Jesus rather than Jesus himself.

Our experiences with God add flesh to the skeleton of our faith. The skeleton—our theology, doctrine, and knowledge of Scripture—gives shape to who we are and what we believe. But a free-standing skeleton has no life. Over time, bones exposed to the elements grow dry and brittle.

Our human flesh and blood, on the other hand, convey life. They protect our bones from breaking and enable us to function and enjoy the life God gives us. But without our skeletal structure, we'd be nothing more than a blob lying on the ground.

If you've built your spiritual life on supernatural experiences and now realize that you were basically a blob with no skeleton, please don't despise your past. Be thankful for those special moments, but remember that they were intended to drive you closer to Jesus. Even now, they can drive you to Jesus, despite taking place months or years ago.

If your walk with God has rarely ventured beyond the safe confines of a dry skeleton, please don't be discouraged. Your lack of an encounter with God doesn't mean he doesn't love you or know who you are. Although space constraints don't allow me to offer any extended words of advice, let me suggest you do what many charismatics have done over the years: tarry.

The word *tarry* is an archaic English word meaning "to wait." In Luke 24:49, Jesus instructed his disciples, "Tarry ye in the city of Jerusalem, until ye be endued with power from on high" (KJV). I quote it in the King James Version because it's the only translation the Pentecostals had at their disposal years ago (and many still prefer that translation today). Taking their cue from this passage, Pentecostals sequestered themselves, either privately or corporately, to wait for the Holy Spirit to endue them with power. All too often we get so busy that we give God little room to interact with us. But the prayer closet has a tendency to shut out the clamor of the world around us so we can listen to that still, small voice.

Sometimes our intense experiences with God change us; other times they act as a momentary spiritual buzz. But in the end, God is after real change . . . which is the subject of the next chapter.

CHAPTER 19

Can You Gimme a Quick Fix?

The Length of Time God Uses to Change a Life

"I can't live like this anymore," the man sobbed, tears streaming down his face. He had come to the altar for prayer after a church service. "For years I've struggled with an addiction to pornography. As hard as I try, I just can't stop. What can I do to get the victory over it?" A devoted family man with a wife and kids, he didn't look like the stereotypical person with a porn addiction—as if there were one.

"Let me pray for you," I offered. For the next ten minutes I rebuked the powers of darkness, the spirit of immorality, and any other spirit I could think of. I bound the generational spirits that might have passed through his family, and then I loosed the spirit of holiness. When we finished, I gave him a hug and prayed for the next person in line.

Did my words make a difference in his life? I don't know. And as much as I believe in prayer (I've written two books on the topic), in retrospect, I should have offered him more than prayer.

A key component of the charismatic movement is the

importance it places on the power of God to transform lives. If you've participated in the charismatic movement, you've likely seen God heal people in a moment. Divine healing is the ultimate in quick fixes.

One minute a wheelchair-bound person can be lowered into a baptism tank and the next minute he can be jumping up and down, a healed man. But does God always opt for the quick fix?

Change Is a Process, Not a Point

When I was a kid, I used to think, *Once I turn sixteen, I'll be a really good Christian.* When I turned sixteen, I thought, *Once I'm twenty-one, then I'll have a really good walk with Christ.* At twenty-one, I thought, *Once I'm married, I'll be a mature Christian.* Then it was when I had kids. Then it was when I turned thirty. Then forty. I'm still waiting for God to get my act together. If God can heal our physical wounds in an instant, why doesn't he heal our emotional wounds or deliver us from our besetting sins in an instant?

Jesus healed people with a touch, but he didn't instantly transform his disciples. Years after Peter denied Jesus three times, he still struggled with fear (Galatians 2:11–14).

Although God has the power to create universes at his command and forever eliminate temptation from the heart of every believer, he doesn't. I find that more times than not, he chooses to change us over a lifetime.

Paul dealt with his personal demons just like Peter. Don't think that after his Damascus road experience he lived a sinless life. The man was opinionated (just ask Barnabas, John Mark, and Peter!) and he couldn't resist speaking his mind before thinking (Acts 23:1–5). Seeing his human side, though, doesn't diminish his credibility. It actually reinforces it, at least to me.

This flawed but brilliant man wrote, "He who began a good work in you will carry it on to completion until the day of Christ Jesus" (Philippians 1:6). Although he was addressing the church in

Philippi, Paul was surely referring to himself, as well. God began a good work in us, but he's not finished! In fact, he's committed to continue working on us for the rest of our lives. What a patient God we have!

Paul furthermore wrote that "we . . . are being transformed into his likeness" (2 Corinthians 3:18). Every believer is in the continual process of being transformed into the image of Christ. We may not be committed to the process, but God is.

Sometimes I wonder if the instantaneous nature of our society feeds our impatience. We like to think that change takes place at a point in time. Once we're lost, but then we're found. We're blind, but then we see. Change, however, is more of a process than a point in time. God is in the process of working in us and through us.

Change Deals With More Than What Meets the Eye

While our bodily ailments may prevent us from living the abundant life, I suspect God takes the state of our heart more seriously than the health of our body.

I must confess that as a charismatic pastor, at times I prayed for a person's instantaneous deliverance because I didn't want to jump into the mess. I wanted God to instantly deliver a man from porn because I didn't want to dirty my hands by touching the wounds in his heart.

Expecting God to instantaneously deliver people from their hurts or sins is a little like treating the symptom rather than the problem. A person I know had a lifelong battle with anger. Although he never physically harmed anyone, his sudden outbursts and periodic tirades prevented him from developing a close relationship with his wife. His children, too, lived in fear of their father's wrath. At times it affected his friendships, and some co-workers felt unsafe when they were around him. "Every day I feel this low-level anger simmering just below the surface, waiting to erupt like a volcano," he once confessed.

How was I taught to deal with this? Rebuke the spirit of anger and then instruct him to confess Scriptures over himself that focus on peace. Above all, he should deny his struggle and repeatedly tell himself, *My mind is controlled by the Spirit, and I have life and peace* (Romans 8:6).

How long should the man do this? Oh, maybe a week or two. If he follows the formula closely enough, he should be able to win the battle.

While many of these actions are good, they don't go far enough.

When the man finally chose to face his issues of anger, he realized that his rage was really rooted in fear. As a child, a few traumatic experiences caused him to become deathly afraid of losing control. When he was very young, some older kids locked him in a playhouse. His immediate emotion was fear, because he felt trapped and couldn't get out. But quickly that fear turned into rage, as he pounded on the doors trying to break out. He felt out of control.

Later, in elementary school, a group of kids ridiculed him on the playground. He tried to make them stop, but couldn't. That same sense of being out of control—because he couldn't make them stop—added fuel to his inner anger.

Throughout his life, even as an adult, whenever people tried to control him or made fun of him, his anger—really his fear—brought back the traumatic emotions from his childhood.

Once he pulled his memories into the light and offered his hurts to Jesus, he began to experience healing. He didn't walk this journey alone; other men joined him. They didn't try to fix him or hold him accountable, rather they simply listened and helped him process through his pain.

Over time his anger began to wane. Are his days of anger behind him? No, but now that his wounds are in the light, his anger doesn't control him like it once did. Periodically, people push his control button and his anger starts simmering again—at times erupting—but the eruptions are much less frequent and less intense. His family likes him a whole lot better, too.

How long did this take? I can't tell you, because his recovery from anger is a lifelong process.

In the same way, I wonder if we do our charismatic friends a disservice by only praying for them. I say "only praying" because people need our prayers, and we need other people's prayers, but we must be willing to do more than that. We need to create safe spaces where we can share the ugly parts of our hearts with each other and enter the mess in others' lives.

Walking With Christ Is So Much More Than Sin Management

At this point, I must add that I realize the solution to our sinful habits and tendencies isn't merely locating the underlying wound and getting it healed. Adam and Eve had the perfect Father (God) and experienced little or no pain and loss (except for Adam's ribectomy episode), and they still sinned. Our struggle with sin follows us throughout our lives regardless of the pain we experience.

As I've explained in earlier chapters, many charismatic churches were heavily influenced by the Holiness movements of the 1800s. Current-day Pentecostals are the grandchildren and great-grandchildren of holiness teachers like Charles Finney, Phoebe Palmer, and Hannah Whitall Smith. These people taught that Christians could reach "entire sanctification." In other words, their hearts could be cleansed of all sin and their default setting would be righteousness rather than wickedness. People who reach entire sanctification are capable of sin, but choose not to.

People's efforts at attaining entire sanctification resulted in a code of conduct that helped prevent them from even catching a whiff of sin. By adhering to this list of behaviors, people hoped it would provide them with a nudge toward their goal. The most notable elements on that list, which have been passed down to us today, are the bans on drinking and smoking. Other practices appear on the list, but drinking and smoking separate Pentecostals from many other Christian denominations. Although charismatics are hard to pin down on the family tree of church history, in many ways they are first cousins of the Pentecostals.

But contrary to the popular belief of many, the Christian life is not defined by our success or failure in eliminating sin. Dallas Willard calls this "sin management." By ridding ourselves of sin, so this way of thinking goes, we become holy people.

God, however, is so much more interested in making us whole than merely delivering us from our iniquities. The Hebrew word for holiness, *qodesh*, means not only "set apartness" but also "wholeness." Becoming whole means becoming who God created us to be, piecing together the fragments of our true selves until they work together again. Holiness, then, includes the healing of our inner selves.

For years the goal of the Christian life seemed pretty apparent: Get rid of sin, speak in tongues, and then you're done. The second part came naturally, but I never quite got it together for the first part.

The Problem With Focusing on Our Sin

"We become what we behold," observed Marshall McLuhan, the noted communications theorist. Over time we take on the characteristics of whatever serves as the focus of our life. Ever notice how some elderly couples look alike? It's because they became what they beheld. What do couch potatoes end up resembling? Potatoes.

Scripture calls this *abiding*. Whatever we abide in, we become. In John 15:5, Jesus said that when we abide in him, we bear much fruit—we become more like him. Jesus' words in all of John 15, in fact, really boil down to this simple phrase: We need to abide in Jesus.

When we make the focus of our spiritual life the eradication or removal of sin, we make sin the focus. In actuality, we're abiding in our flesh, that part of us that craves sin. So it's no surprise when we become further entrapped by it.

If I'm struggling with lust and trying not to think lustful thoughts, what am I focusing on, or abiding in? My lust. The same applies to anger or greed or materialism or selfishness.

This truth even applies to losing weight. I once tried one of those high protein diets where I could eat all the meat and cheese my stomach desired—the kind of diet all men should thrive on. But despite my penchant for meat and cheese, all I could think about was salad and bread. Five days later, I couldn't take it any longer. My obsession for what I couldn't have drove me to break my diet.

Whatever I focus on becomes an object of worship. An idol. If I make finances the focus of my life—maybe I'm not making enough, maybe I just want to make more—then finances become my idol.

But it works the same way with love. If I'm focusing on becoming a more loving person, who or what am I focusing on or abiding in? Myself. In the end, I simply become more self-absorbed and more frustrated because I'm not becoming a more loving person.

How Change Happens

John the apostle understood this when he wrote, "He who keeps [Christ's] commandments abides in Him, and He in him" (1 John 3:24 NKJV). The people who keep Christ's commandments are the ones who abide in Christ.

No magic pill exists for people who want to change. And God is too great for us to place limits on the endless ways he can change people. But I cannot ignore the reality of this truth: We become what we behold, or to put it into biblical terms, we become what we abide in.

What do we do to change? Virtually nothing. We cannot change ourselves. We can remove the sources of temptation and the triggers that cause our downward slides, but we cannot change ourselves. Only God can change us.

Look closely at this passage of Scripture:

> I appeal to you therefore, brothers, by the mercies of God, to present your bodies as a living sacrifice, holy and acceptable to God, which is your spiritual worship. Do not be conformed to this world, but be transformed by the renewal of your mind, that by testing you may discern what is the will of God, what is good and acceptable and perfect.
>
> ROMANS 12:1–2 (ESV)

My friend Frances has pointed out to me that in this passage, the main thrust of Paul's appeal centers around two passive verbs. If you're rusty on your English grammar, all you need to know is that a passive verb doesn't do the action, it receives it. Just think of the passive husband who sits around all day waiting for his wife to tell him what to do. A passive husband is the embodiment of the passive verb.

The passive verbs in this passage are "be conformed" (we're not supposed to do that), and "be transformed" (we're supposed to do that). J. B. Phillips famously paraphrased the first passive verb this way: "Don't let the world around you squeeze you into its own mold." But how are we supposed to "be transformed"? Paul commands his readers to be transformed, but how can they be transformed if the transforming work must be done to them?

All we can do is present ourselves to God. We present ourselves like the priests used to present the sacrificial bulls and sheep before God. Fortunately, God isn't going to roast us on the altars like he did back in the day. But he wants us to present ourselves to him.

We offer all that we are—body, mind, and spirit—to God. *This* is spiritual worship. But we present ourselves not to an uncaring God whose only intent is to rid us of our despicable sins; we present ourselves to the God who sent his only Son to lay down his life on the cross for you and me. We present ourselves to the God who longs to commune with us, to abide in us and us with him. "Let him who boasts boast about this: that he understands and knows me, that I am the Lord" (Jeremiah 9:24).

Deeper than a psychological problem, our sin is a spiritual problem. Counselors can help us identify the problem, but they can't necessarily offer the solution—apart from Christ.

You and I face a constant bombardment of messages about how to change: All we need is more education or an experience with God or accountability relationships or the spiritual disciplines. Or we just need to try harder. None of these will work!

Change, in fact, isn't about you. It's about Christ in you! It's not about becoming a different person; it's about becoming who you really are because your identity is Christ! He is the deepest part of you.

The kind of change God is after in you and me cannot take place in an instant. We cannot become like Christ in an instant. But deeper still, we cannot know Christ in an instant. I've been married for twenty years and I feel like I'm just getting started on knowing my wife. How much more so is this true in our relationship with Christ? Abiding in Christ is a lifelong journey.

When we seek the quick fix, we shortchange ourselves on God's lifelong pursuit to make us more like his Son. And the more we become like his Son, the more we take pleasure in being with him. Our relationship changes from asking him for answers to our requests to enjoying the nuances of a dynamic relationship—which is something every believer seeks.

Now that we've looked at how God changes us, let's explore how God changes the world through us by prayer.

CHAPTER 20

My Kingdom Come, My Will Be Done

The Intersection of Our Desires and God's Plans

In the movie *Bruce Almighty*, almighty God gives godlike powers to Bruce Nolan (played by Jim Carrey) over a limited area in Buffalo, New York. Intoxicated with his omnipotence, Nolan recreates his world to his own advantage. He transforms his beat-up car into a high-powered dragster with a license plate that reads "Almityl." Then, doing his best Moses imitation, he parts the bumper-to-bumper traffic so he can screech through the sea of cars unobstructed. Then he takes revenge on a gang that beat him up a week before.

In one telling moment, he proclaims, "I am Bruce Almighty. My will be done."

Later, God (did you know he carries an amazing resemblance to Morgan Freeman?) confronts Bruce Nolan for misusing his powers. "I had to take care of a few things," Nolan answers with a degree of defensiveness. "I righted a few wrongs in my own life first."

Ripped From the Pages of Bruce Almighty

"Power corrupts. Absolute power corrupts absolutely," the historian Lord Acton once wrote. Knowing the power of heaven and earth lies at our disposal is pretty heady stuff. Dispensationalists don't wrestle with the fallout of knowing they can access the Holy Spirit's power to make a tangible change in their world. Charismatics, on the other hand, know it and sometimes take full advantage of it.

One day a pastor and I walked to an ice cream shop, and because it was a beautiful day, we decided to enjoy our ice cream at the outdoor patio. While we were sitting at our table, some rain clouds gathered overhead and it started to sprinkle.

"I come against this rain in the name of Jesus," the pastor prayed with a measure of certainty.

"Why did you do that?" I asked.

"Well, we're enjoying our ice cream, and I don't want the rain to ruin our time outside."

"Are there farmers in the area?"

"Yes, of course."

"Then why is it more important for us to enjoy our ice cream outside than it is for the farmers to get the rain for their fields?"

"I'm just confessing that it won't rain on us," he volleyed back.

Charismatics believe fervently in the power of prayer. For the most part, we jump at the opportunity to participate in citywide prayer gatherings. We read books about prayer and attend conferences on prayer. And why not? If you believe that the Holy Spirit is actively at work in the world today, you know that your prayers make a difference—which they do.

From a young age we were taught how to pray and how not to pray. For instance, we were warned that when we pray, we should never utter that ultimate faith-killer: "If it's your will."

When praying for a person's healing, we should never pray, "Lord, if it's your will, please heal Uncle Harold of his irritating bunion."

Or "Dear God, Laura is really unhappy with her job and now she's applied for work at Mega Telephone Company. We plead with you to open the doors of heaven and grant her the job, if it's your will."

Instead, many of us were taught to pray, "I come against the spirit of foot bunions in the name of Jesus. God, shod his feet with the preparation of the gospel of peace and heal Uncle Harold right now!" Or we should pray, "God, I call out to you on Laura's behalf that you will give her the coveted Director of Chair-Warming position at Mega Telephone Company. Lord, move her name ahead of all the other candidates so the employers will give her the job."

Just *Who* Is Prayer All About?

Looking back, I was pretty confident about God's will. Basically, God's will was identical to mine. If I wanted a new computer, God must want me to have a new computer, too. While in college, if I spotted a pretty girl on campus, whom I wanted to date, then God must have saved her just for me. Oh yeah, God answered that one!

In prayer, we stood on verses like John 14:14 ("You may ask me for anything in my name, and I will do it") and John 15:7 ("If you abide in Me, and My words abide in you, ask whatever you wish, and it will be done for you" NASB).

Actually, we didn't really pray, not in the traditional sense. We held God to his Word or his promise. When praying for Uncle Harold, we could hold God to Isaiah 53:5, "By His stripes we are healed" (NKJV). For Laura, we could pray Proverbs 12:2, "A good man obtains favor from the Lord." Basically, any Scripture remotely connected to the need could be used in prayer to hold God (hostage) to his Word.

Why did we pray this way? I can't answer for others, but I can answer for myself. I wanted to be in control, I didn't trust God to act in my best interests, and I thought I knew better than God what my needs were.

At the time, I didn't realize the implications of holding God to his promise. It implied if I didn't hold him to his promise, he wouldn't keep it. That he was a promise breaker and that he wasn't inherently good. That if I wasn't looking out for myself, nobody else would . . . certainly not God. This kind of thinking lends itself to being very demanding and self-absorbed—because if God won't look after my best interests, then no one else will, except me.

When she was two or three years old, my daughter Allison used to pray like this: "I pray Allison, I pray Allison, I pray Allison, I pray Allison." At first, her prayer made me laugh, but over time my wife and I realized she needed to expand her world by just a little bit. Actually by a lot! However, the tendency for all of us is to pray in that same vein, we just make it sound a little more dignified.

You can tell a great deal about people's walk with God by listening to their prayers.

- Does their prayer consist solely of asking God for stuff?
- What are the most frequently used words—I and me or you and your?
- Who does most of the talking?
- Who calls the agenda and issues the commands?
- Why do they pray?

The answers to these questions reveal the difference between seeking the kingdom of *God* and seeking the kingdom of *me*.

It All Depends on Your Definition of Good

As much as we may be tempted to believe that God wouldn't give us good things if we didn't force his hand, Jesus says otherwise:

Which of you, if his son asks for bread, will give him a stone?
Or if he asks for a fish, will give him a snake? If you, then,

though you are evil, know how to give good gifts to your children, *how much more will your Father in heaven give good gifts to those who ask him!*

God will give us *only* good gifts! Every good and perfect gift comes from God, James 1:17 tells us. God spoke through the prophet Jeremiah, saying that he rejoices in doing us good (Jeremiah 32:41). God doesn't begrudgingly give us good things. He takes joy in sharing himself with us.

The question is who gets to decide the definition of good? A "good" dinner in the eyes of my two youngest daughters, Allie and Marina, consists of a hearty helping of potato chips rounded off with as many chocolate chip cookies as will stay down.

My wife, Kelley, once brought four-year-old Allie to the doctor for an immunization. Although no shot had ever frightened her before, at that moment the thought of a nurse sticking a two-inch needle into her arm terrified her.

As the nurse inched the syringe closer, my frightened daughter screamed and ran out of the room. For the next few moments, the nurse and my wife chased Allie throughout the doctor's office, into the lobby, and out the front door—much to the amusement of the people cheering little Allie on.

Was the shot good? Not in Allie's eyes—and it didn't feel good when the needle poked her in the arm. But in the eyes of the nurse, and to Kelley and me, yes, the shot was very good. It likely prevented her from suffering a much more painful fate of measles or rubella.

In *Bruce Almighty*, God grants Bruce Nolan the responsibility of answering the multitudinous prayer requests of the people in Buffalo. As the requests begin to mount, Nolan tries unsuccessfully to develop a system to answer the many needs. Exasperated, he decides to answer everyone's request.

What happens? A man suddenly grows taller and a woman

loses forty-seven pounds on the Krispy Kreme donut diet. And eleven hundred people win the lottery, with each person receiving a payout of only seventeen dollars. Outraged, the city of Buffalo erupts into a riot.

Funny, giving people what they want only results in people becoming increasingly self-absorbed.

Later Bruce and God discuss the cause of the riot.

"I just gave them what they wanted," Bruce reflects.

"Since when does anyone have a clue about what they want?" God answers.

Oscar Wilde once wrote, "When the gods wish to punish us they answer our prayers." Sometimes, the worst thing that can happen to us is for God to grant our requests. We may not understand why God denies us, but if he is good and he can only give us good gifts, he deserves our trust—even if it brings us more pain or more stress.

This we know: It's okay to ask. Jesus said, "Ask, and you will receive, that your joy may be full" (John 16:24 NKJV). Paul encouraged his readers that in anything and everything, they should present their requests to God (Philippians 4:6). Their requests, not their demands.

To reiterate John Wimber's words from chapter 15, "I don't know why God heals sometimes and other times he doesn't. All I know is that people get healed more often when you pray for them than when you don't." Regardless whether our request is big or small, God encourages us to ask. The worst he can do is say no.

The Bible translates a variety of Greek words for "pray." Not coincidentally, each word—*proseucho, deomai, aiteomai,* and *erotao*—means to ask or request.

Our Desires Reveal the Condition of Our Hearts

So it's okay to ask. But then we must ask ourselves, *What am I asking for?* A few years ago I ran across a quote from Augustine of Hippo, the great church father who lived from AD 354 to 430. This great man once wrote, "A longing desire is always praying, though the tongue is silent. If you are ever longing . . . you are ever praying. When does prayer sleep? When desire grows cold."

Prayer begins at a much deeper place than the words we speak. Paul explains that we groan inwardly as we await the redemption of our body. But he explains further that the Spirit intercedes with groans that words cannot express (Romans 8:23, 26).

Where does prayer begin? According to Augustine, it begins with desire. More than words, our desire communicates the true longing of our heart. Jesus said that out of the overflow of our heart, our mouth speaks (Luke 6:45).

So if someone were to ask you, "What is your deepest desire?" how would you answer?

- To get out of debt?

- To be released from your dead marriage?

- To become independently wealthy?

- To enjoy one day of relief from your physical or emotional pain?

- To be used of God to impact your world?

Although these desires aren't necessarily sinful or wrong, and God certainly wants the best for us, perhaps his refusal to grant our requests is intended to bring us to the end of ourselves. Once we come to the end of ourselves, we have nothing . . . no one . . . but him.

Now let's turn the tables on this question. What does God want our desire to be? Let me offer a few suggestions that come to mind:

- To bring him glory.

- To see his kingdom come.

- To spend time with him without ulterior motives.

- To know him.

To know someone, in the biblical sense, means more than the exchange of facts and information. Knowing God goes deeper than gaining a firm grasp of the finer points of Scripture and theology. The biblical sense of knowing someone implies not only sexual intercourse, but the union of two people into one.

The clearest example of this in Scripture can be found in Jesus' words in John 15:

> I am the vine; you are the branches. Whoever abides in me and I in him, he it is that bears much fruit, for apart from me you can do nothing. . . . If you abide in me, and my words abide in you, ask whatever you wish, and it will be done for you. By this my Father is glorified, that you bear much fruit and so prove to be my disciples.
>
> JOHN 15:5, 7–8 ESV

The other day while meditating on this passage, I asked myself, *Christ lives in me, but do I live in him?* I'm relieved knowing that Jesus living in me isn't contingent on my living in him. So often during the day, I desire temporal things that likely won't even catch my fancy in a week or two. I settle for the temporal when I could live with—better yet, live *in*—the eternal. Jesus wants to be my desire; he wants me to want him.

To live in Christ, to yearn only for him, to commune with him, and to rely only on him—that's what it means to abide. And when I abide in him, when his words abide in me, then I can ask whatever I wish and he will give it to me. But my desires will inevitably change as he becomes my one desire.

What God Wants Along With Our Desire

One other aspect of desire that I so easily overlook: Not only does Jesus want to be my *desire*, but he also wants to be my *delight*. During a heartfelt discussion with my wife a few years ago, she commented, "Mike, I wish you would enjoy me." Her words cut to my heart. I wanted to be with her, but I didn't necessarily enjoy being with her. That was a turning point for me.

In the same way, God wants us to want him, to be *with* him, to be in him. But he wants us to enjoy him, as well. The Westminster Confession of Faith states that the chief end of man is to glorify God and enjoy him forever. When we enjoy God, we can't help but glorify him, as well.

Psalm 37:4 tells us, "Delight yourself in the Lord and he will give you the desires of your heart." When I delight myself in the Lord, my priorities change. I become so enamored with God that I lose my taste for the things that promise to satisfy me but can't.

Where does our charismatic experience intersect with this? Our intimate experiences with the Holy Spirit should serve as an invitation to enter the loving dance of the Trinity. Rather than establish ourselves as people of power, we would do better to focus ourselves on an ever-increasing abiding relationship with Christ.

When God becomes our desire and delight, we forget about ourselves. In fact, we trust him so completely that we see no need to fend for ourselves. We laugh at "holding God to his Word" because we know his heart—he would never leave us nor forsake us. He will only do what is good for us and in us.

Prayer isn't a laundry list, nor is it a means to merely get what we want from God. It assuredly includes our requests, but more than that, prayer is an invitation into rich, satisfying intimacy with the Father, Son, and Holy Spirit.

CHAPTER 21

What the Devil Is Going on Here?

Spiritual Warfare: Our Part and God's Part

Since our journey of significance is rapidly coming to an end, it's time for another charismatic quick quiz. Please place a check mark under the appropriate column according to the degree that you think the following statements, terms, or concepts are supported by Scripture:

Statement, Term, or Concept	Supported by Scripture	Kind of Supported by Scripture	Not Supported by Scripture	Huh?
1. Lucifer was once the head worship leader in heaven.				
2. Territorial spirits				
3. God has given us the authority to bind and loose principalities and powers.				
4. Spiritual mapping				

Statement, Term, or Concept	Supported by Scripture	Kind of Supported by Scripture	Not Supported by Scripture	Huh?
5. God and Satan are engaged in a cosmic battle.				
6. Our participation in this cosmic battle determines the outcome.				
7. Strategic level spiritual warfare				
8. Demonization				
9. Through Adam's sin, Satan gained authority to rule over this world.				
10. Armor of God				
11. Psycho-demonic spiritual cleansing				

Short answers:

1. Kind of supported by Scripture, but it's a stretch (Isaiah 14; Ezekiel 28).
2. Kind of supported by Scripture (Daniel 10).
3. Not supported by Scripture.
4. Neither the term nor the practice has clear scriptural support.
5. Not supported by Scripture.
6. Not supported by Scripture.
7. Not supported by Scripture.
8. Supported by Scripture (Matthew 8:28–34, among many).
9. Not supported by Scripture.
10. Supported by Scripture (Ephesians 6:11–18).
11. Huh? I made that one up!

Some of these comments are discussed more fully in this chapter. For even more discussion, go to *www.strangefireholyfire.com* to debate it, discuss it, or offer your own perspective.

Just because it isn't mentioned in the Bible doesn't make a practice wrong or sinful. But it should put the practice in its proper place. Had it been important enough, God surely would have found someplace in Scripture to adequately explain it.

A Frank Introduction to Spiritual Warfare

In 1988, Frank Peretti, a former Assemblies of God pastor, wrote a novel entitled *This Present Darkness*. Initially, sales of the book were slow. But aided by the exuberant recommendations of Amy Grant and Michael W. Smith on their concert tours, sales began to skyrocket. The book has reportedly sold 2.5 million copies and continues to sell well today.

Peretti's well-written fictional account tells the story of a pastor and a newspaper reporter who prevent a New Age society from covertly taking over a small town and its college. As the story unfolds, the reader witnesses cosmic battles between armies of angels and demons over their divinely assigned territories.

Charismatics raved about the book because it explained many of their experiences with spiritual warfare. The book also introduced spiritual warfare to non-charismatic evangelicals eager to enlist in the battle.

Charismatics and non-charismatics alike began using *This Present Darkness* as a manual on prayer, exorcism, and spiritual warfare. "Prayer cover" and "territorial spirits" found their place in the charismatic lexicon as a result of this book. Before the book's release, few talked about the reality of territorial spirits, but after the book, the idea of angels and demons overseeing a city, region, or country was regarded as truth. Why? Because *This Present Darkness* said so.

Although spiritual warfare was alive and well among charismatics and Pentecostals before its release, the book created an insatiable thirst for more knowledge about the subject. And thus the spiritual warfare cottage industry began. As this movement coalesced, Dr. C. Peter Wagner emerged as its leader. Wagner's scholarly credentials and position as professor of church growth at Fuller Theological Seminary in Pasadena, California, brought credibility to the movement. I studied under Wagner at Fuller in the early 1990s while the spiritual warfare movement was taking shape.

Under Wagner's apostolic leadership, spiritual warfare conferences began sprouting from the soil, watered by Peretti's book. These conferences took the reality of demonic forces seriously and positioned believers on the front lines of the spiritual battle between light and darkness.

The Good in the Spiritual Warfare Movement

Most informed evangelical and charismatic discussions involving demonic activity begin with C. S. Lewis's famous opening words to *The Screwtape Letters*:

> There are two equal and opposite errors into which our race can fall about the devils. One is to disbelieve in their existence. The other is to believe, and to feel an excessive and unhealthy interest in them.

Have you ever noticed that both extremes view themselves as representatives of the "balanced position"? Christians who claim to believe in a real Satan yet live as if he doesn't exist maintain that they represent the biblical approach. On the opposite end of the continuum, spiritual warfare mercenaries who seemingly fight demons on every side claim that they don't look for demons under every rock. But turn your back to them and they probably will!

Charismatics believe so strongly in the unseen power of God that it shouldn't come as a surprise that they believe just as strongly in the unseen powers of darkness. The greatest argument for the existence of Satan can easily be seen in the daily newspaper. Tragedies like 9/11, the Oklahoma City bombing, ongoing terrorist threats, the tragic battles in Darfur, even the Columbine High School massacre (located only three miles from my home) prove that Satan exists. On a personal level, agree to step into Christian leadership and immediately you'll sense an invisible target on your back.

To borrow from Hal Lindsey's bestselling book from the 1970s, Satan is alive and well on planet earth. The father of a good friend of mine—a pastor—was killed by a satanist. And without going into details, one of my closest friends embarked on a satanic confrontation as a teenager and soon thereafter left the faith. In my opinion, his unpreparedness for the battle served as his undoing.

Anyone who denies the reality of the demonic hasn't read the Gospels closely enough. Jesus preceded the inauguration of his ministry with a foray into the wilderness, where he was tempted by the devil. From then on, he continually healed people harassed and/or controlled by demons.

From Adam and Eve's introduction to the serpent in the garden to Satan's defeat as seen in Revelation 20, Scripture clearly teaches that a spiritual battle rages around us.

At the time that the spiritual warfare movement was beginning to flourish, Western society was operating from a very modernistic worldview. If something couldn't be scientifically proven, it didn't exist. Otherworldly powers fighting cosmic battles seemed far-fetched, even among many Christians.

Perhaps the success of *This Present Darkness* could be partly attributed to its function as a wake-up call to the church. Satan is alive and well (maybe not well—because his fate is sealed). Dark powers *do* exist. For this reason, I'm grateful to people like Frank Peretti, Peter Wagner, and Cindy Jacobs for reminding the church that the god of this age—Satan—has blinded many people to the Good News of Jesus Christ.

> And even if our gospel is veiled, it is veiled to those who are perishing. The god of this age has blinded the minds of unbelievers, so that they cannot see the light of the gospel of the glory of Christ, who is the image of God.
>
> 2 CORINTHIANS 4:3–4

Anyone who spends time in Peter Wagner's presence can't help but like him. When he tells his corny jokes, this self-deprecating man laughs the loudest. But even more so, they can't deny his deep desire to see people give their lives to Jesus. He and others in the spiritual warfare movement infused many unassuming believers with a passion for the lost and a renewed emphasis on prayer. Prayer walking has become a normal facet of the prayer ministry of many churches—charismatic or not. And Wagner's book *Prayer Shield* helped me realize my deep need for prayer.

I once invited anyone from my congregation to join me in attending one of Wagner's spiritual warfare conferences. A handful of people were interested, including a man who had just begun attending my church. Little did I know that he wasn't a believer . . . yet. At the conference he gave his heart to Jesus. Upon our return home, he became my most adamant prayer supporter. He organized a prayer room in my church and embarked on his own prayer walks.

Becoming a believer at a spiritual warfare conference produces a unique strain of Christian. It means that the spiritual warfare gene gets added to the person's spiritual DNA, which can be good . . .

Do We Really Want to Stir Up All the Powers of Evil?

. . . and bad.

Young David may have defeated Goliath with only a slingshot, but few battles are won without the appropriate protection gear and training. Confronting the powers of hell presents a challenge to even the most mature Christian. But throwing a young believer into the battle is a recipe for disaster.

During that time, I led my congregation into a spiritual battle when I wasn't prepared—nor was my congregation. The week I called my church into concerted prayer for our community and into the battle, all hell broke loose. A family informed me they were leaving the church because we were too evangelistic. An incident occurred in the church during my sermon that eventually threw my congregation into controversy and division. The fallout of the incident contributed to my premature resignation two years later. I then left pastoral ministry for two years just to recover from the experience. My young believer friend still loves Jesus, but his war wounds from that controversy left him disillusioned with the church.

I learned an important lesson as a result of my experience: Don't stir up the powers of evil when you lack spiritual maturity—both in yourself and in your congregation. Looking back, I even question the wisdom in stirring up the spiritual powers in my community.

Leanne Payne, a modern-day mystic whose teachings on prayer and inner healing have impacted thousands of charismatics and non-charismatics alike, voices similar concerns. In her book *Listening Prayer*, she describes an incident involving a group of people who approached her about praying for one of her upcoming meetings. Leanne met with the intercessory prayer group, but when they began to pray, the group confronted the principalities and powers over the meetings she was about to hold.

Leanne reflects on this experience:

> [The prayer group] had drawn the attention of the dark powers toward the body of Christ in that place by *praying to them* and pridefully seeing themselves as "binding" them. As it turned out, they became a channel through which a "principality and power"—a ruling spirit over that city—descended into our midst. It was one meant to be withstood in spiritual battle only

by the holy angels as we battled properly for the salvation of souls. . . .

Needless to say, we were brought into a spiritual conflict of unusual proportions, one that need never have occurred. These folk, thinking they were intercessors, had merely succeeded in informing the powers of darkness in, over, and around that city that we were coming! In listening to them proudly relate all the hair-raising tussles with dark powers, I realized they take this "gift" every place they go. The way they pray assures that the people they are involved with will have dramatic and terrible confrontations with evil powers, and that some of them will come under serious demonic deception. This is a dangerous error.

Perhaps our spiritual confrontations with principalities and powers stir up needless trouble and heartache. It's kind of like the smart-alecky little kid who challenges the neighborhood bully and his minions. He may have confronted the bully and delivered a few punches, but he gets smacked down in the process. Sometimes the little kid even delivers the knock-out punch, but more times than not, he just gets beaten up. It's a high price to pay, too high in many cases.

This brings us back to the idea of God being all-powerful, all-wise, and all-good. If God is all-powerful, then the battle belongs to whom? God.

> This is what the Lord says to you: "Do not be afraid or discouraged because of this vast army. *For the battle is not yours, but God's.*"
>
> 2 CHRONICLES 20:15 (ITALICS ADDED)

All too often, my need to be important drives me to fight the battle on God's behalf. I bind the powers of darkness, and as a result, reap more trouble upon myself.

Payne further explains, "In showing us how to pray, the

Scriptures record no one focusing on demons. Rather, it is as Christ taught us to pray: 'But deliver us from the evil one.' In other words, 'You do it, Lord.' "

People in the spiritual warfare camp point to Daniel 10 as evidence of territorial spirits and the role of prayer in combating them. Daniel received a revelation from God but didn't understand what it meant. He fasted and prayed for three weeks but still no answer came.

Finally, an angel appeared, explaining that the prince of Persia had prevented him from giving Daniel the interpretation to the dream. The conflict grew so fierce that Michael the archangel had to step into the conflict in order for the angel's message to get through.

Does this passage prove the existence of territorial spirits? Probably. Although with such scant evidence in Scripture, I would hesitate from giving it undue importance in my faith.

Proponents of strategic level spiritual warfare encourage believers to engage the principalities and powers in battle, yet Daniel wasn't even aware that a battle was being fought in the heavenlies. He was a bystander, not a participant in the battle.

Scripture never gives us an example of a mortal confronting a territorial spirit. They likely exist, but it doesn't appear that God has called us to fight them.

Let's Not Give the Devil His Due

Although no biblical evidence exists of people confronting the powers, we can find plenty of examples in Scripture of godly men and women co-partnering with God in delivering people from demonic oppression. Even then, we must be cognizant of the extent of demonic influence.

Years ago my father was praying for a person after church. Suddenly the person fell to the ground, writhing and making strange sounds. He and a few others took authority over the evil spirits and pleaded the blood of Jesus, but the writhing and mumbling continued.

My father then realized the man was in diabetic shock! Someone called an ambulance and the man was taken to the hospital. It just goes to show that it's not always a demon hiding under that bush. More than freedom from demonic oppression, the man needed some orange juice!

In fact, it seems to me that we give Satan way too much credit—credit that he wants, but doesn't deserve. It's easier to blame Satan for a spirit of immorality or a spirit of gluttony rather than shoulder the blame ourselves. To be honest, my flesh doesn't need much help from Satan. He may cooperate with it, but I don't need any assistance in really messing things up.

Furthermore, we give Satan too much credit in the cosmic battle between darkness and light. When I served as a foot soldier in the spiritual warfare movement, I implicitly assumed that the victory depended upon the perseverance and prayers of the saints. If believers failed to mobilize and diligently engage in the battle, the battle would be lost, Jesus wouldn't return, and Satan would be given more time to wreak havoc on souls who would otherwise be won for the kingdom.

This type of thinking assumes that God and Satan are equal adversaries. But nothing could be further from the truth! The battle is over! At the cross, Jesus defeated the power of sin, death, and Satan. Paul wrote,

> When you were dead in your sins and in the uncircumcision of your sinful nature, God made you alive with Christ. He forgave us all our sins, having canceled the written code, with its regulations, that was against us and that stood opposed to us; he took it away, nailing it to the cross. *And having disarmed the powers and authorities, he made a public spectacle of them, triumphing over them by the cross.*
>
> COLOSSIANS 2:13–15 (*ITALICS ADDED*)

At the cross, Jesus not only defeated Satan, but he disarmed the very powers and authorities that spiritual warfare advocates unceasingly oppose. To focus our spiritual lives on an "ongoing" spiritual battle demeans the victory Jesus won on the cross. The early church battled demonic powers over individuals, but they celebrated the victory of Jesus over the enemy of our souls. Author Gustav Aulen comments, "The work of Christ is first and foremost a victory over the powers which hold mankind in bondage: sin, death, and the devil."[1]

Before the cross, Satan couldn't even exercise ultimate authority over this world. "The earth is the Lord's, and everything in it, the world, and all who live in it," the psalmist declares (Psalm 24:1). Through their sin, Adam and Eve couldn't grant Satan authority over this world because the authority wasn't theirs to give. Only God holds the right to grant authority to any person or force, and any influence Satan has, ultimately has been given to him from above (John 19:11). Martin Luther once astutely observed, "Even the devil is God's devil."

If charismatics knew that the battle was already won, would they take on the principalities and powers? Of course not. They wouldn't need to. In the words of Leanne Payne, our responsibility is "mop-up action."

For people who strongly believe in the power of God, I was perplexed by hints of deep fear among certain leaders in the movement. One day I happened to be driving by the headquarters of a ministry on the front lines of the spiritual battle. Seeking to get an endorsement from the ministry's leader for a book I was writing, I decided to drop in.

But after entering their building, I couldn't find their office. Round and round I walked through the hallways only to find locked doors without any signs. Eventually I discovered that the headquarters was unmarked and only accessible with a pass card. No one explained their reasoning, but my guess is they wanted to prevent their satanic counterparts from engaging in a physical confrontation. Do we need to live in fear like this? Absolutely not.

Who Fights the Battle?

But most important, setting the sights of our spiritual lives through the lens of spiritual warfare directs our attention to the wrong person. Our faith doesn't rest on an ongoing battle against someone, it rests on Jesus—he is the point, not Satan.

Let's jump back to chapter 19 for a moment and return to our discussion about abiding. If you remember, I explained that whatever we abide in, we become. When we abide with Christ, we become more like him. Conversely, when we focus on overcoming our sin, we abide with our sin and actually become more entrapped by it.

In the same way, when we make spiritual warfare the focus of our lives, who do we abide in? Satan and the powers of evil. We overcome principalities and powers not by fighting the darkness, but by walking in and with the light.

Here's how James explains it:

> Submit yourselves, then, to God. Resist the devil, and he will flee from you. Come near to God and he will come near to you.
>
> JAMES 4:7–8

Although James is giving us a short list of commands, the context tells us that we resist the devil by submitting to God and drawing nearer to him.

Furthermore, Jesus said, "Now is the time for judgment on this world; now the prince of this world will be driven out. But I, when I am lifted up from the earth, will draw all men to myself" (John 12:31–32). Satan, the prince of this world, is driven out as Jesus is lifted up. When we place too much emphasis on spiritual warfare, we lift up Satan. If I were Satan—and thank God, I'm not!—I would be repulsed by people fixated on Jesus.

The favorite passage of most believers who engage in spiritual warfare at any level is Ephesians 6:10–18. In it, Paul lists the armor of God. What do all the pieces share in common? They represent Jesus!

- Jesus is our belt of truth (John 14:6)
- Jesus is our breastplate of righteousness (2 Corinthians 5:21)
- Jesus is our gospel of peace (Ephesians 2:14)
- Jesus is our shield of faith (Hebrews 12:2)
- Jesus is our helmet of salvation (1 Thessalonians 5:9)
- Jesus is the Word of God (John 1:1, 14)

When we put on the armor of God, we put on Jesus. We cannot defeat the Enemy, but Jesus can and already has!

When offering advice for overcoming the darker sides of our sinful nature, Paul exhorts us to clothe ourselves with Christ. (See Romans 13:14.)

Martin Luther, the great reformer, penned what might be the greatest hymn ever written. Although he faced fierce satanic opposition, he fully understood who wins the battle.

Below, I conclude this chapter with the powerful words to his great hymn *A Mighty Fortress*. The lyrics could serve as a summary of this chapter. Please read them slowly and take a moment to reflect on their meaning, especially in relation to God's, and our, involvement in the battle.

> A mighty fortress is our God,
>   A bulwark never failing;
>   Our helper He amid the flood
>   Of mortal ills prevailing;
>   For still our ancient foe
>   Doth seek to work us woe;

His craft and power are great,
And armed with cruel hate,
On earth is not His equal.

Did we in our own strength confide,
Our striving would be losing;
Were not the right Man on our side,
The Man of God's own choosing;
Dost ask who that may be?
Christ Jesus, it is He;
Lord Sabbaoth, His name,
From age to age the same,
And He must win the battle.

And though this world, with devils filled,
Should threaten to undo us,
We will not fear, for God hath willed
His truth to triumph thro' us;
The Prince of Darkness grim,
We tremble not for him;
His rage we can endure,
For lo, his doom is sure,
One little word shall fell him.

That word above all earthly powers,
No thanks to them, abideth;
The Spirit and the gifts are ours thro'
Him who with us sideth:
Let goods and kindred go,
This mortal life also;
The body they may kill:
God's truth abideth still,
His kingdom is forever.

CHAPTER 22

Removing Your Label From Your Lapel

The Future of the Charismatic Movement

Years ago, my father's job in the oil business required that he spend part of his day researching court records in county courthouses. At that time he was working in rural Texas. And the congenial person that he is, he convinced the county clerk to lock him into the records vault during the lunch hour—while the rest of the courthouse was closed.

One day he decided to peek at the lunacy files from the court records of the early 1900s. He was astounded as he read some of the far-fetched measures public officials had taken to declare certain undesirables insane. Of course, knowing that he was in Texas, it shouldn't come as a surprise.

An entry dated between 1910 and 1920 read something like this: "On November 10, Billy Joe-Bob Henry engaged in a conversation with John Franklin at the corner of Live Oak and Center Street. Mr. Henry emphatically shared with Mr. Franklin that the preceding night he had received the Holy Ghost and spoken in other tongues. Mr. Franklin reported Mr. Henry's exuberant behavior to

Sheriff Roscoe Jenkins, who filed a lunacy petition and admitted Mr. Henry to the insane asylum."

In the early days, claiming to be filled with the *Holyghost* (if you speak Pentecostal, you say Holy Ghost as if it were a one-syllable word) could get you branded a heretic at best and a lunatic at worst.

Even as late as the early 1970s, Pentecostals and charismatics struggled to find acceptance in mainstream society. A friend once confessed to me that during the Jesus People Movement, the army discharged him because he mentioned to a commanding officer that he spoke in tongues.

For many of us, our first encounter with the Holy Spirit—what many consider being "filled with the Spirit"—brought dramatic changes to our lives. Some of us gave up drugs. Others stopped sleeping around. Marriages were restored. People were delivered of destructive habits. We experienced a new sense of peace and freedom. As a result, we couldn't help ourselves—all we wanted to do was share the gift that had been given to us.

Despite our desire to be accepted, and probably due to a little strange behavior on our part, mainstream churches forced us out on our own. In the earlier days, the Pentecostals formed their own denominations, such as the Church of God in Christ and Assemblies of God. The charismatic renewal of the early 1960s (for a refresher on who is who, go back to chapter 1) produced similar results, but instead groups formed independent churches of their own.

But something tells me God isn't finished. . . .

Mother Knows Best

Thirty years ago, while I was in my early teens, my mother commented to me, "Someday, people won't distinguish between charismatics and non-charismatics, because all the spiritual gifts will be accepted in every denomination." It didn't make sense at the time. Mainstream churches in the 1970s forcibly offered the left hand of fellowship to countless pastors and everyday believers who advocated the practice of all the gifts of the Spirit. But she was right.

Renewal movements that affirm all the charismatic gifts are alive and well in virtually every Christian denomination, even the Southern Baptists—which means that Hawaii has frozen over!

According to a 2008 Barna study (*www.Barna.org*) entitled "Is American Christianity Turning Charismatic?" 36 percent of Americans claim to be charismatic or Pentecostal Christians—up from 30 percent only ten years ago. Nearly half of all adults (46 percent) who attend a Protestant church are charismatic. Barna defines a charismatic or Pentecostal Christian as a person who claims to have been "filled with the Holy Spirit" and believes that "the charismatic gifts, such as tongues and healing, are still valid and active today."

Reflecting on current cultural trends that affirm personal expression and diverse emotions, George Barna comments, "It is not surprising that the Pentecostal community in America has been growing—nor do we expect it to stop making headway."

That twentieth-century phenomenon called dispensationalism is slowly dying with nary a whimper. In the same way, so are the distinctions that define a charismatic from a non-charismatic. Barna further offers this perspective on these increasingly blurred lines:

> We are moving toward a future in which the charismatic-fundamentalist split will be a historical footnote rather than a dividing line within the body of believers. Young Christians, in particular, have little energy for the arguments that have traditionally separated charismatics and non-charismatics. Increasing numbers of people are recognizing that there are more significant arenas in which to invest their resources.

My mama was a prophet!

A New Kind of Charismatic

While mainstream churches are integrating charismatic practices, independent charismatic churches seem to be working hard to remain a "peculiar people." They chase trendy theologies and become increasingly addicted to hype.

Tom Freiling, the former publisher of a charismatic publishing house, whom I quoted in chapter 9, once commented to me that from his perspective: "Charismatic churches seem to be getting more extreme in order to distinguish themselves from the mainstream churches who have accepted charismatics."

Perhaps because we've grown accustomed to being different, we feel the need to continue being different. Even if it means becoming more extreme.

So what does the future hold for independent charismatics? If they continue trying to be peculiar, they'll eventually fade away into oblivion, because the mainstream churches will offer something more grounded and palatable to society.

So what is my dream for the independent charismatic church? If I were the first pope of the Independent Charismatic Network of Churches, I would recommend the following:

Return to your first love.

Many renewal movements begin with innocence and a burst of enthusiasm, but over time they grow overweight, lazy, and self-absorbed. Every renewal movement eventually needs more renewal. We're fooling ourselves if we think we don't need it as well, because we do!

The church in Ephesus played a pivotal role in the New Testament church. Initially, Jerusalem served as the hub of the Christian faith, but then it moved to Antioch, and eventually Ephesus. At different times, Paul, Timothy, and then John made Ephesus their base of ministry operations. Through the ministry of the church of this once-great city, missionaries were sent throughout the Roman Empire, and everyone in Asia heard the gospel (Acts 19:10).

The churches in other cities looked to the Ephesians for leadership. They respected and emulated this influential church for their vibrant ministries and perseverance in the face of persecution. But within fifty years of their birth, they needed a rebirth. In his first letter to the seven churches in Asia, Jesus addressed the Ephesians:

> Yet I hold this against you: You have forsaken your first love. Remember the height from which you have fallen! Repent and do the things you did at first. If you do not repent, I will come to you and remove your lampstand from its place.
>
> *REVELATION 2:4–5*

Despite their good works and noble intentions, Jesus said they had lost their first love. This shouldn't come as a surprise, because all of us tend to lose sight of what's important. We get focused on working for Jesus rather than focusing on Jesus. We enjoy the gifts of the Spirit so much that we stop sharing them with people outside our circle. And over time, we forget what brought us to Jesus: love. So how do we return to our first love?

First, Jesus directs the Ephesians to remember. Do you remember the joy of discovering that Jesus not only loves you, but he likes you, too? Do you remember the innocence of those earlier times and the steadfast belief in God's ability to do anything? Remember the joy of serving Jesus, sharing Jesus, and being used by Jesus, without thought of receiving anything in return? Most of all, do you remember what it was like to enjoy just being with Jesus?

Again, if I were pope of the Independent Charismatic Network of Churches, I'd recommend that every believer in our churches take a personal inventory and reflect on questions like these.

Although the 1960s and '70s were far from perfect (if you

dealt with the control issues in the shepherding movement, you heartily agree), the focus of our earlier days centered on knowing Jesus better and being used of God. Many of the teachings today seduce us with self-absorbed promises that only feed our flesh.

My disillusionment with the charismatic movement resulted from seeing our overall focus change from Jesus to self. And I must be the first to admit that I did the same thing. I used God as a means to get what I wanted, and I sought the Holy Spirit in order to get a spiritual buzz.

But God didn't pour out his Spirit on believers so we could get a spiritual buzz and spend our evenings watching Christian television. Nor was it a way for us to discern the mind of God so we could fill our homes with more stuff.

To gain a little perspective on what it means to live as a Spirit-filled believer, as pope, I would make books available written by earlier charismatic leaders. Authors would include the likes of Smith Wigglesworth, Dennis Bennett, Derek Prince, Francis MacNutt, and Mel Tari. I'd also expose our people to precursors of the charismatic movement like Andrew Murray and Phoebe Palmer. Authors like these would help us remember to fulfill the Great Commandment of loving God and loving our neighbors (Luke 10:25–37).

Second, Jesus encourages the Ephesians to repent. Repentance means to change our mind and actions. To turn in the other direction. We must own our condescension, exclusiveness, materialism, and narcissism and ask God for forgiveness—preferably in public forums. Fortunately, the blood of Jesus covers even the deepest stain. If you can remember a person whom you've offended or overlooked in a narcissistic binge, then seek the person's forgiveness.

Third, Jesus tells the people to repeat the things they did at first. When you first fell in love with Jesus, what did you do? Returning to our first love means to do the things we did at first.

Let's return to the Word of God and pursue an ever-deepening relationship with the Word made flesh—Jesus. Let's look for the hidden gifts of grace that God blesses us with every day, and let's share them with others. By forgetting about ourselves and giving our lives for others, we become the people God intended us to be.

Create accountability structures in our independent churches and ministries.

My heart ached when Ted Haggard, the pastor of New Life Church in Colorado Springs, fell. But I was also thankful for the accountability structure he had already set in place. Before his fall, Haggard described, to anyone who would listen, the checks and balances in his church . . . and they worked!

Too many independent charismatic churches, however, haven't followed Haggard's example. Senior pastors shouldn't be allowed to milk their congregations so they can live elaborate lifestyles, nor should they be allowed to set up family businesses that use their churches as cash cows. Any person who pursues a pastoral or ministry leader position with the desire to get rich is a charlatan.

While independents abhor the idea of confining themselves to denominations, denominations do provide structures that prevent fraud, immorality, and wacked-out theology from continuing. Some charismatics might find it difficult to believe that the Holy Spirit can work through denominational churches as well as independent churches, but it's true.

While a step in the right direction, apostolic networks haven't proven to me that adequate checks and balances are in place. Who are the apostles accountable to? And if they're accountable to a board, who decides who will sit on the board?

The greatest need in the charismatic movement is for independent ministries, especially television ministries, to make themselves accountable to someone. Anyone. I applaud Lee Grady and *Charisma Magazine* for exposing the excesses of these ministries.

Perhaps someday they can make a very public call to all these ministries to gather together for a very public discussion on accountability. Then they can covenant together to make changes to their culture and bylaws that ensure they uphold their commitments.

Join with other believers who worship differently than you.

Every city has only one church—with different expressions, which we call congregations. When Paul wrote his epistle to the Ephesians, he wasn't addressing a particular church, like the Ephesian Family Worship Center. He was addressing the scattered house churches (some as large as two hundred) throughout the Ephesus metropolitan area. Did all the house churches look alike? Highly unlikely.

An often-overlooked ministry of the Holy Spirit is unity. Paul exhorted the church in Ephesus to "Make every effort to keep the unity of the Spirit through the bond of peace" (Ephesians 4:3). Let's prayerfully shorten our list of essential beliefs and adhere to them, but then let's work alongside other churches (even non-charismatic ones), so the world will see Jesus, and not division.

Move charismatic from a noun to an adjective.

As I mentioned in chapter 2, Scripture never refers to a contingent of Jesus' followers as charismatics. The New Testament refers to them as "disciples," "believers," and to a lesser extent, "Christians" (which today is a loaded word in itself).

When people ask me if I'm a charismatic, I'm not sure how to answer. I fit George Barna's definition—I'm filled with the Spirit (I offer that as a statement of faith) and I validate all the spiritual gifts—but they sure don't define me. That's why I've removed the charismatic label from my lapel. Our spiritual practices shouldn't define us—because Jesus should. Identifying myself as a charismatic just feels . . . awkward.

Most people know that a noun is a person, place, or thing. Like labels, nouns define us. If you call yourself a charismatic, you're using the word as a noun. But what if we chose to use the word as an adjective? An adjective describes a noun. For example, I live in a beige house. I don't live in a beige; beige adds color (literally!) to the description of my house.

If charismatics moved the word into the adjective position, then what would they be? Not charismatics, but charismatic disciples of Jesus, charismatic followers of Christ. The word now adds color to our definition, but it doesn't define us.

Someday, I hope the distinction between charismatics and non-charismatics fades so much that no one will be able to tell the difference. At that point, we'll be brothers and sisters in Christ, whom the Bible refers to as Christians. That feels much better.

Well, that brings us to the end of our pilgrimage, our journey of spiritual significance.

I'd like to close by offering this prayer for you:

Heavenly Father, I thank you for our time together. Without a doubt, some of the ideas I have presented in this book fell short of your desires. Would you help my readers separate the wheat from the chaff? In the same way, Holy Spirit, I invite you to come alongside my readers and help them separate the wheat from the chaff of their uneven charismatic experience. The grass withers, the flower fades, but your Word will stand forever. Guard them and guide them by your Word.

In the same way, we lift up this divine move of God we call the charismatic movement. Despite its excesses, we acknowledge that through it, and in spite of us, it is a sovereign move of your Spirit. Thank you for the leaders who have brought us this far. We pray that you would raise up more leaders who will draw us closer to your heart and to you. Please give all of us a keener sense of truth, and a greater distaste for anything flavored with self.

May your kingdom come and your will be done on earth as it is in heaven. In the name of the Father, the Son, and the Holy Spirit. Amen.

Thank you for joining me. I hope we journey together again.

Good Mourning, Holy Spirit

Moving Forward in Light of Your Charismatic
Experience

Like death and taxes, you can pretty much expect that when you
involve yourself in the life of a church, you *will* get hurt. All of
us want to believe that churches act in the best interests of others and that our leaders operate with God-honoring intentions.
We want to believe that everyone who loves Jesus will agree. But
they don't.

Even when we resign ourselves to its inevitability, the pain of
disappointment or abuse or loss or abandonment or embarrassment
can be debilitating and overwhelming. The resulting fallout can
leave us disillusioned with the church and angry at God.

In the midst of writing this book, my church experienced a
tumultuous upheaval in leadership that resulted in a church split.
Both the people who left and the ones left behind felt angry and
confused. Small groups disintegrated and longtime friendships
came to an end. Due to the resulting financial shortfall, a third
of our church staff was let go. And after a great deal of prayer,
I resigned from my position as an associate pastor. My greatest

sorrow is that countless people departed, vowing never to return to the church.

Perhaps a similar experience with a charismatic church prompted you to read this book. How do we find healing? How do we avoid becoming jaded or embittered by our experience? At times the pain can be so unbearable that we'd rather die than continue.

But in actuality, death is the pathway to the healing we seek. We must die to our expectations, our illusions, our disillusions, and our dependence on others. We must die to our deep need for others to fill the hole that only God can fill.

Joy Comes in the Mourning

The default setting in most people is fixed on the belief that death is bad. It's the end as we know it—which is true. Most people who don't know Jesus live in fear about what comes next. The best they can hope for is a bright light that they run to . . . and then who knows what happens next. Either that or they look forward to oblivion. Nothingness.

Death forces us into finding a new normal, a different way of living in light of the past. This journey of discovery is called mourning.

Now, there's good mourning and there's bad mourning. Bad mourning can mean getting stuck in the past without finding your way into the present. I once knew a woman whose husband had died twenty years ago. But listening to her, you would think he was still alive. Somehow his name came up whenever we talked.

Bad mourning can also mean living in bitterness over the hurts of the past. In the church I recently left, I co-taught our quarterly new members class. Usually at some point during our four weeks together, I shared my story. Often, someone would pull me aside afterward and confide to me their experience of being burned by the charismatic movement. One time a couple confessed with tears in their eyes, "Our charismatic church hurt us so bad that we stopped going to church for twenty years. This is our first time back."

But there's also *good* mourning. Good mourning means facing the past, assessing the loss, and finding significance as a result of the experience. Now, that doesn't mean the pain goes away completely. But it does mean working through the wounds one-by-one.

Good mourning results in a new life that exists after the death. We don't ignore the events of the past, nor do we stow them away as painful reminders in the back of our dusty closet of secrets. On the contrary, they become an active part of our story. In fact, our life wouldn't be the same without it. We wouldn't want to go back to those days, but we live without regrets.

Good Grief

If you've suffered pain as a result of your involvement in the charismatic movement, I'd like to offer you some ideas to help you move forward. Please don't consider these exhaustive or definitive. They more or less result from my varied painful experiences in the church. As you embark on this foray, bring your Bible and a journal and pen (unless you like to journal on your computer like I do). Below are some ideas to help you move forward in your grief:

1. *Take inventory of your past.* Reflect on your charismatic journey. What was good and what wasn't so good? Who was helpful and who was hurtful? How have your experiences shaped you both positively and negatively? What stones of remembrance do you have as a result of your journey? What stones need to be disposed of in order for you to move forward?

2. *Feel it.* As you continue journaling, place yourself in some of your most vivid, positive memories. How did it feel? How do you feel now as you reflect on them? Now do the same with your most vivid, painful memories. Feel the pain. Our tendency is to move away from the pain and numb ourselves through denial, addictions,

anger, or an assortment of other emotions—but do what you can to stay in the pain. If you need someone to talk you through it, go ahead. Often, the painful memories overwhelm us when we least expect it. If you're in the middle of doing something when it catches you by surprise, stop, identify the emotion, and invite the Holy Spirit into your memory. Later, reflect on your experience and add it to your journal.

3. *Look for glimpses of God.* Read through your journal and ask God, "Where were you in my story?" Try to avoid limiting his involvement only to positive experiences, because God can, and often does, appear in our most painful or humiliating moments. Then wait, and listen.

4. *Express your gratefulness.* Look over your list of people whom God used to positively impact your life (from #1). Are there any other people missing, perhaps people who both hurt you *and* helped you? You may be surprised as you discover that God used flawed individuals to also make a significant impact in your life. Take a few moments to thank God for the good he worked in you because of them. You may even want to take a moment to send a thank-you note to the various people who impacted you, describing how God used them to show you more of Jesus.

5. *Acknowledge your brokenness.* Perfect churches don't exist, and neither do perfect people. Leaders make mistakes just like you and I do. And as long as you and I are a part of it, the church will be imperfect. As you reflect on your painful or disappointing memories, how did your shortcomings, issues, mistakes, or brokenness contribute to your painful memories? What would you do differently if you knew then what you know now?

6. *Forgive.* Forgiveness is more a process than a point in time, so make sure you take the time you need on this step. In light of #5, you may likely discover that you need forgiveness, too. The realization that we need God's forgiveness serves as the best reason for us to forgive others (Matthew 18:21–27). Take a moment and ask God to forgive you, and thank him for sending Jesus to provide

you with the means to be forgiven. In light of your prayer, and as you feel God bringing healing to your heart, forgive. You may only be able to start with one offense, but that's okay. Start with one and then build momentum. Sometimes the best you can do is pray, "Father forgive them, for they know not what they do." When you're ready to take another step forward, pray, "Father, I forgive that person." Lewis Smedes once wrote, "When we forgive, we set a prisoner free, and discover that the prisoner set free is us."

7. *Give.* This may be the most important step. Look over your work up to this point and give it to God. Offer him your pain, embarrassment, and memories, both good and bad. Any time a painful memory hits you, pray something like this: "God, I don't want to carry the pain of this memory any longer, nor do I want to walk in unforgiveness, so I give it to you." If it helps, visualize yourself piling everything into a gunnysack or a pillowcase and offering it to God. You may even want to write up a list of everything you are offering to God and then set fire to it, symbolizing your inability to take it back. At that moment, your strange fire becomes holy.

Notes

Chapter 1

1. Grant McClung, "Pentecostals: The Sequel," *Christianity Today*, April (2006), 30.
2. Stanley M. Burgess and Eduard M. van der Maas (eds.), *The New International Dictionary of Pentecostal and Charismatic Movements* (Grand Rapids, MI: Zondervan, 2002), 35, 277.

Chapter 4

1. Philip Schaff, *The Nicene and Post-Nicene Fathers: Second Series Vol. I*, Eusebius: Church History, Life of Constantine the Great, and Oration in Praise of Constantine (Oak Harbor, WA: Logos Research Systems, 1997), 3.
2. Johannis Lukawitz, "Waldensis Confessio," 1431. Secured through Google books, A.J. Gordon, *The Ministry of Healing* (London: Hodder and Stoughton, 1882), 79.
3. Stanley M. Burgess and Eduard M. van der Maas (eds.), *The New International Dictionary of Pentecostal and Charismatic Movements*.
4. Cornelius J. Dyck, *An Introduction to Mennonite History* (Scottdale, PA: Herald Press, 1993).

Chapter 6

1. Larry Mullen, Jr., quoted in *U2 By U2*, ed. Neil McCormick (New York: HarperCollins, 2006), 117; quoted in Steve Stockman, *Walk On: The Spiritual Journey of U2* (Orlando, FL: Relevant Books, 2005), 16–27.

Chapter 9

1. Thomas Freiling, in discussion with the author, December 17, 2007.

Chapter 14

1. Reiko Myamoto Dewey, "More Messages in Water: The Spirit of Ma'at interviews Dr. Masaru Emoto," *http://www.life-enthusiast.com/twilight/research_emoto.htm* (accessed March 3, 2008).

Chapter 15

1. Ronald A. N. Kydd, "Healing in the Christian Church," *International Dictionary of Pentecostal and Charismatic Movements*, ed. Stanley M. Burgess and Eduard M. van der Maas (Grand Rapids, MI: Regency/Zondervan, 2002), s.v. "Healing in the Christian Church".

Chapter 18

1. Walter Hollenweger, July 12, 1993, lecture notes from *Charismatic Problems and Promises*, Fuller Theological Seminary.

Chapter 21

1. Gustav Aulen, *Christus Victor: An Historical Study of the Three Main Types of the Idea of Atonement*, trans. A. G. Herber (New York: Macmillan, 1977), 20.

About the Author

Michael J. Klassen is the co-founding pastor of The Neighborhood Church in Littleton, Colorado, and The Neighborhood Church Network, a newly forming movement of micro-churches consisting of two hundred to four hundred people who love God and love their neighbors as themselves. Values of this movement include experiential corporate worship, lifelong spiritual transformation, congregation-based ministry, vibrant community, missional living, and viral church planting. For more information, visit *www.myneighborhoodchurch.org*.

He is the author of three books, including *Prayers to Move Your Mountains* (Thomas Nelson), and has worked on a variety of Bibles, including the *Women of Faith Bible*, the *Prayer Bible*, and the *New Men's Devotional Bible*. He has also written eight books in collaboration with other authors, and enjoys coaching aspiring writers.

Michael has enjoyed twenty years of marital bliss with his wife, Kelley. They live in Littleton, Colorado, with their three daughters, Anna, Allison, and Marina.

You're invited to enter into a conversation about *Strange Fire, Holy Fire*. Learn more about the book, read Michael's blog, interact with *Strange Fire, Holy Fire*, and join an ongoing discussion with other recovering charismatics at *www.strangefireholyfire.com*. Michael is also available for speaking engagements, retreats, and for preaching in church worship services. You can contact Michael at his Web site.